QUIET STRONG

First African American
Explosive Ordnance Disposal Diver

Based on the Life of
Master Chief Boatswain's Mate Sherman Byrd

Cynthia Byrd Conner

Let It Flow Publishing Company

Quiet Strong

Based on the Life of Master Chief Boatswain's Mate Sherman Byrd

Some names and identifying details have been changed to protect the privacy of individuals.

CLEARED For Open Publication, Department of Defense, OFFICE OF PREPUBLICATION AND SECURITY REVIEW, OCT 19, 2017, 17-S-2222

Let It Flow Publishing Company

Paperback ISBN: 978-0-9977906-9-6

Hardback ISBN: 978-0-99779-068-9

eBook ISBN: 978-099779-062-7

PRINTED IN THE UNITED STATES OF AMERICA

TABLE OF CONTENTS

ACKNOWLEDGMENTS 1

INTRODUCTION 3

THE ANCHOR 5

CALL IT LIKE YOU SEE IT 21

THE GO-GETTERS 35

EYES FOR A SAILOR 45

THE APPLE DON'T FALL FAR FROM THE TREE 57

PHYSICAL SCREENING TEST 73

BUY-IN (DEEP SEA DIVERS SCHOOL) 83

A MOMENT OF CHOICE 99

EXPLOSIVE ORDNANCE DISPOSAL 109

QUIET STRONG 121

THE GOAT LOCKER IN THE CROSSHAIRS 131

WHILE YOU WERE SLEEPING 139

THE CUBAN MISSILE CRISIS 145

CHIEF IN HIS GRASP 151

BIBLIOGRAPHY 157

AUTHOR AFFILIATIONS 163

ACKNOWLEDGMENTS

With special thanks:

Oh God, thank you for entrusting me with this divine assignment and giving me the wisdom, strength and patience to accomplish it. To Jesus Christ, my Savior and Lord, I dedicate this book to you.

To my father and mother - without whose unconditional love, integrity, courage, and selflessness I would not have been inspired to write this biography.

To my siblings Sherlyn, Sherman Jr., Azelle, Yolanda, Sandra, Andre, and Laurie - thank you for encouraging me, loving me, and praying for me. I love you more than you may ever know!

To my husband Alton - I remember the words we put on the back of our wedding program, those words still ring true after 34 years; "It is a beautiful thing to know that you are in the will of God, rejoice with us for we know!" I am so glad that God chose to make us one. I love you. Thank you for all of the things that you do!

To my daughter Crystal and my son Maurice - thank you for believing in me. I thank God for blessing me with the two of you. You bring me joy. I love you so much!

To my nieces and nephews - thank you for inspiring me to leave you this legacy with the hope that you will aspire to make your grandparents proud. I love you dearly!

To my Aunts, Uncles, and Mother-in-law, thank you for your unwavering love and guidance along the way. You have taught me so much! I will always love you!

To all of my cousins - the Byrd, Keys, White, Arnold, and Brown clan, I thank God for each and every one of you. There are no family reunions like our family reunions! I pray that God will give us the strength to keep them going so we may continue to pass down our family history from one generation to another. See you soon! Love ya cuz!

To BM3 Sidney Crudup II - thank you for sharing your knowledge and experiences as a Boatswain's Mate in the United States Navy with me. You were the missing link that I needed to bring Dad's story full circle. Thank you for your service to our country!

To Sonja Newbill - thank you for your expertise and patience in helping me to complete and publish this book. Your kindness is greatly appreciated. May God continue to bless you to help other authors get to the finish line.

To Charles Collins III, owner of Azure Aesthetics - I am awed by your talent! The book cover is so powerful! Thank you for your vision. My family and I are truly grateful for all you have done for us!

To MMC (EOD) Ret. Mike Coulter - thank you for being the Explosive Ordnance Disposal (EOD) subject matter expert for this book. Your knowledge of the history of EOD and your ability to share it in layman's terms has helped me to grasp the magnitude of the EOD warrior's sacrifice. Our family greatly appreciates you keeping the memory of our father alive. Last but not least, thank you for your service to our country!

INTRODUCTION

A teenager, tired of living by Jim Crow laws in the southern state of Mississippi, seeks to find out God's purpose for his life. The youngest son of sharecroppers, Sherman Byrd watched and waited for a sign. A series of events pointed him in a direction few Negroes had travelled before. Death loomed all around. Determined to walk by faith and not by sight, Byrd's journey unexpectedly led him down a path where he became a pioneer in one of the most dangerous jobs known to mankind. Disarming bombs!

A silent oath, a vow unspoken, explosive ordnance disposal divers do not tell war stories. It is the Sovereignty of God that unleashes truth that cannot stay buried beneath the test of time. Selfless sacrifices and epic feats burst forth like lava from a volcano. Now, is the appointed time to share the life story of Master Chief Boatswain's Mate Sherman Byrd, the first African American Explosive Ordnance Disposal Diver in the United States Navy.

CHAPTER ONE

THE ANCHOR

It was the anchor that caught the corner of his eye, as he walked briskly past the U.S. Navy recruiter's table. There it was, smack dab in the center of a white cap, strategically placed on top of a stack of books. The anchor looked brand new, although the silver streaks in the recruiter's hair clearly told the story of years of dedicated service. Gold and silver, strong and sturdy, the hooks of the anchor seemed to plunge into his heart. After all, that is what an anchor does. The sudden and violent descent could be appeased only by embedding in the sand or rocks at the bottom of the water. The anchor was content to fulfill its God-given purpose, steadying a ship that wants to drift. Something inside the 17-year-old eighth grader stirred. He felt a connection. It compelled him to turn around and walk back toward the table. Oh, how Sherman Byrd longed to fulfill his God-given purpose. If only he knew exactly what that purpose was.

As he approached the Navy recruiter, their eyes met awkwardly. Awkward, because the darkness of his skin did not repulse the recruiter, as it did so many of the local white men in Greenwood, Mississippi. Sherman lowered his head, as he had done on thousands of other occasions. Colored men in Mississippi had been lynched for far less offenses than locking eyes with a white man. Jimmy Jones had been found hanging from a tree just last month. Nobody seemed to know how he got there. The word around town was that Mr. Green, the old man who owned a couple of hundred acres of land, paid money to have Jimmy lynched because he called him by his first name, "Peter."

Jimmy was only 20 years old.[1] The recruiter smiled as the young man approached the table. The anchor did exactly what it was supposed to do. It hooked another one.

World War II had ended. A U.S. containment strategy against Soviet Union Communist expansion, regarded as the Cold War, had begun. Registering men for the Selective Service was no longer required. The culmination of the draft created some new issues for the Navy. A huge personnel turnover was about to occur. Hundreds of thousands of previous enlistments were about to expire. According to Vice Admiral William M. Fechteler, deputy chief of Naval Operations personnel, 232,000 regular enlistments would begin to expire in January 1948. The Navy would need to recruit 13,000 enlistees per month to offset this projected turnover.[2] It was late September 1947. The Navy recruiter knew he needed to make good use of his time.

Competition for new recruits became fierce because of the enactment of the National Security Act of 1947. The War and Navy Departments combined to become the National Military Establishment, which in turn created the Department of the Air Force.[3] The recruiter knew that the earlier bird catches the worm and local high schools were full of young men ripe for the picking.

The mere thought of enlisting 13,000 recruits each month put a smile on Yeoman Chief John Henry Johnson's face. After all, he was a salesman. Before joining the Navy in 1927, he had earned a decent living selling H. C. Hollinger products in Jackson, Mississippi. Most housewives would purchase a bottle of H. C. Hollinger pain-relieving liniment to keep on hand for the various aches and pains experienced by the family.

Chief Johnson stood five feet, nine inches tall, with eyes as blue as the ocean. His athletic build was similar to a long-distance runner, and he was quite conscientious of the first impression portrayed to possible Navy recruits. He wanted to display the confidence of the World's greatest Navy in the way he walked and talked. Possession of a good sense of humor, and genuine love for his country, combined to make him a successful recruiter. Meeting a recruitment quota was not his main focus. It was more about assessing whether a young man had the character traits to exemplify the honor of wearing a Navy uniform. Scuttlebutt about President Harry S. Truman desegregating the U.S. Armed Forces was popping up everywhere. Nothing was in writing. Change is not swift or comfortable, but it has to start somewhere. Chief Johnson knew the road that Negroes would have to travel to have a successful career in the Navy. It would be difficult but beneficial at the same time. As these thoughts sped through Chief Johnson's head, he almost did not want to persuade this young man to join the military. Maybe he should wait a couple of years, to give desegregation a chance to flourish.

An easel off to his left-hand side displayed a poster listing eight benefits of joining the Navy. Men would have an honorable career, with an opportunity to advance to a chief petty officer (CPO), the highest enlisted rate. They would serve on modern Navy ships and visit foreign lands. More than likely, this young man had never been out of the state of Mississippi. It would be an opportunity for him to educate himself and to learn a trade. If Chief Johnson could not get a recruit to sign on the dotted line with these first five benefits, he would pull out his ace cards. The Navy could offer Negroes access to medical treatments, healthy food, and liberal pay. Negroes were earning $3.50 a week working all day in the cotton fields. Chief Johnson was prepared to offer a recruit $75.00 a month. [4] That was more than five times what many currently were being paid.

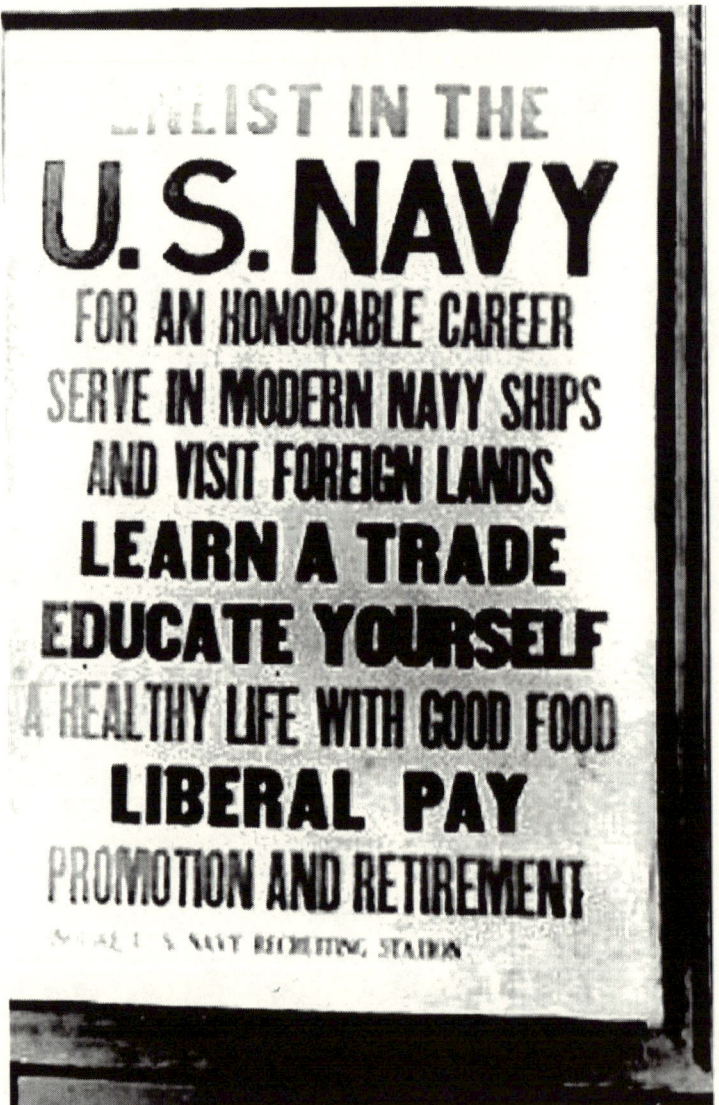

Join the Navy
Photo Courtesy of the United States Navy

Most recruiters did not actively pursue the enlistment of Negroes because they thought that the majority could not read or write. They were right. Why waste their time? Reading and writing were prequalification requirements needed to join the Navy.

Chief Johnson however had noted the conviction and urgency in which the Negro teachers at Stone Street High School, Home of the Fighting Tigers, taught. The teaching did not stop in the classroom, it continued down the hallways, on the football field, and spilled outside at the end of the day. Teachers persistently corrected foolish behavior, encouraged those with hung-down heads, and infused hope in the hopeless. They held the students to high academic standards, teaching life skills, such as typing and carpentry. It was okay to dream, and the students started to do just that. Life beyond the cotton fields was possible. Learning how to read and write was their first step to finding it. Joining the Navy could very well be their second.

Chief Johnson looked at Sherman's hands as he approached the recruiting table. Amazing life stories are told in the appearance of a person's hands. It was socially unacceptable for a white man to shake a Negro's hand. Jim Crow laws of etiquette were practiced religiously in the South. [5] Chief Johnson thought that it was one of the most ridiculous things he had ever heard. He was born in Jackson, Mississippi, and was nourished on the breast milk of a Negro nanny. Employed as a wet nurse, the nanny was kind to Johnson and his two sisters. [6] They grew up loving her as if she were family. It baffled him how it was considered unclean to shake a Negro man's hand, but he could drink a Negro woman's breast milk.

Chief Johnson assessed that Sherman was a sharecropper. His outer hands were rough and pricked around the fingernails by the bolls of the cotton plant. His inner hand was calloused, from the frequent gripping of the wooden handle of a hoe. Sherman's hands were large and strong, indicative of long work hours and heavy lifting. Chief Johnson checked off one of the four things he listed in his head when evaluating possible new recruits: Yes, he seemed healthy enough to complete the physical rigors of Navy boot camp. Three more checks on the list to go. Was he interested in the Navy as a career? Could he read and write? Was he 18 years old?

The recruiter introduced himself, "Hi, I am Yeoman Chief John Henry Johnson. What is your name, young man?" Never before had a white male recognized Sherman as a young man. If he had a penny for every time he had been called "Hey boy," he would have a sizeable chunk of change. It caught him off guard but he quickly recovered and said, "My name is Sherman Byrd."

That was all Chief Johnson needed to know before he started to talk to him as if they had known one another for years. Chief Johnson was a polished storyteller and took pleasure in explaining the reasons why a person should join the Navy.

Chief Johnson said to Sherman, "The window of opportunity is right in front of you. All you have to do is sign on the dotted line."

Opportunity. Now that was a familiar word. Mrs. Hattie Baker, Sherman's eighth-grade English teacher, had taken the time to explain to her students the true meaning of the word opportunity. It was different from the definition found in Webster's Dictionary. Mrs. Baker was a Christian. She loved the Lord Jesus Christ with all her heart and gladly would tell you so if you so much as slowed down while passing her in the hallway. The students had nicknamed her "Holy Roller," but they only would call her that when she was well out of hearing range. Sherman chuckled to himself. He had been one of the main ringleaders in these shenanigans. Webster defined opportunity as "an amount of time or a situation in which something can be done." [7] Mrs. Baker adamantly disagreed. A no-nonsense instructor, she demanded excellence from each and every one of her students. Sherman envisioned her even now. There she stood, tall and slender, around five feet, seven inches. Her voice, strong and dignified, thundered like a seasoned orator. At the end of every class, Mrs. Baker with her chestnut-complexioned skin and shoulder-length hair pinned up in a bun would stand in a posture as if she were about to recite the Pledge of Allegiance. Then she would bellow out, "Now remember class, opportunity is the appointed time of an event pre-planned by Almighty God. It requires an act of faith. When the window opens, jump through it!"

As Sherman listened to the recruiter, he began to grasp what Mrs. Baker had said. Joining the Navy was his window of opportunity. The recruiter's stories about visiting foreign countries and being surrounded by nothing but water for days with no land in sight had provoked his imagination.

He still wanted to know the story behind the anchor. Sherman pointed to the hat on top of the stack of books and asked Chief Johnson to tell him about the anchor. Chief Johnson adjusted his posture, stood shoulders squared, and looked him directly in his eyes: "This is the Fouled Anchor. It is the symbol of the U.S. Navy Chief Petty Officer. It represents the trials and tribulations encountered day by day. The letters U.S.N. are boldly placed across the shank of the anchor. The U stands for unity, reminding chiefs that they must cooperate, maintain harmony and continuity of purpose while taking action. The S stands for service to a True and Living God, our fellow man, and our Navy. The N stands for navigation. It is a constant reminder to keep ourselves on course. We must walk upright before God and man in our relations with all mankind, especially our fellow chiefs. A chain is entwined around the shank and flukes of the anchor. Symbolizing the flexibility, we must maintain during life. Forging each link of the chain, we move forward with Honor, Morality, and Virtue. Last but not least, the Anchor is emblematic of the hope and glory of the fulfillment of all God's promises to our souls. Oh, how golden it is. Oh how precious is the Anchor by which we must be kept steadfast in faith, encouraged to abide in our proper station amidst the storm of temptation, affliction, and persecution." [8]

Sherman was mesmerized, not only by the words that Chief Johnson spoke but by the principle and passion that accompanied it. He shivered. This was it, God's will for his life, the path that he should follow. Sherman needed to hurry off to class, but with cheer he told Chief Johnson that he would return after school to talk with him a little more.

The rest of his day in school went by like a blur. He could not wait to go back to the Navy recruiter's table to inquire more about the advantages of joining the Navy. Thoughts of being paid $75.00 each month turned over and over in his mind. He would be able to send money home to his mother for her care and save money to be used to better his future. Saving money was hard, at least from the Byrd family's perspective. Years of working diligently and faithfully in the cotton fields had yielded them no money to save. His family barely broke even year after year.

Something within him said, "Go." He embraced it. He felt it was a calling. The rest of the world may not see him that way. Most whites did not want colored people in the Navy. They could not imagine having to eat, sleep, shower, and use the same toilet. That did little to discourage Sherman. He had come of age.

Sherman met with Chief Johnson on several occasions over the course of the next three months. Chief Johnson verified that he could read and write. Sherman said that he was interested in the Navy as a career and provided verification of his age. The chief informed him that he must obtain his parent's permission to join the Navy and be enlisted as an apprentice seaman. Chief Johnson patiently answered Sherman's questions. Even if he had the time, he knew that answering all of the young man's questions would never happen. So, he did the next best thing. He explained to Sherman the meaning behind the tradition of "Ask the chief." It was the responsibility of the chief to stay on top of everything connected to his rating. As the supervisor, he must train the young men assigned to him. If a time came when Sherman did not know something, he wanted him to make sure that he would find the chief and ask him. The chief would know the answer.[9]

Joining the military was a good option for a young colored man living in the South. Sherman was born in Carrollton, Mississippi, and went to school in nearby Greenwood. Staying in Mississippi was far too dangerous. The state of Mississippi had more documented lynchings of colored people than any other state.[10] Only God knew the number of the undocumented ones. Although Sherman's three older brothers served in the U.S. Army, he had his reasons for not following in their footsteps. Sherman had a deep love for the water and was a strong swimmer. It seemed as if he belonged there. So a career in the U.S. Navy would be a perfect fit. Therefore at the age of 17 years old, and with his mother's permission, Sherman volunteered to join the U.S. Navy. He trusted God and jumped through his window of opportunity.

It was the day after Christmas in 1947 when the bus pulled into the station in Greenwood, Mississippi. Two separate ticket windows were marked: one for white people, the other for colored. Apprentice Seaman Sherman Byrd was accepted at the Naval Recruiting Station Satellite, Greenwood, Mississippi, and was on his way to enlist at the Naval Recruiting Station, Little Rock, Arkansas. Dressed to combat the teeth-chattering conditions in Greenwood, Sherman was glad that he was headed west. His recruiter informed him that he would do his basic recruit training at the Naval Training Center (NTC), San Diego, California.

News that a blizzard hit the Mid-Atlantic States was abuzz at the station. Local newspapers had labeled it the Great Blizzard of 1947. Central Park, New York, was buried in 26 inches of snow. Buses and cars were trapped; businesses were closed. People were dying. The storm had not been forecast and caught residents by surprise.[11]

It was 38°F in Greenwood. Sherman felt fortunate.[12] He was about to relocate to a place with an average temperature of 70°F. It would be the start of a new journey for Byrd, commencement of a new life as a Navy sailor.

Byrd was not alone. He enlisted under the Buddy Program with his cousin Calvin "Butter Roll" Brown. Sherman and Butter Roll were best friends. Their mothers were sisters and the boys grew up together. Both young men were eager to find their seats on the bus. It would only be a few more minutes before they pulled out of the station.

Sherman was ready for this new life even though it meant leaving his mother behind. It was Annie Lloyd Keys Byrd who prayed for her children to be able to rise above the poverty of the cotton fields of Mississippi. She would encourage them when times were tough by saying, "the Lord will make a way somehow." She was right. The Lord had made a way.

To Sherman, sailing on a U.S. Navy ship was an opportunity of a life-time. He would see places he had only heard about in school. Leaving his mother however weighed heavy on his heart. Annie Lloyd had experienced great difficulty in raising her family by herself. Sherman's father Loyd Byrd, was in and out of their lives. His absence troubled Sherman. Loyd viewed the cheap labor of colored people picking cotton as an advantage to the white man. He did not care much for picking 200 pounds of cotton per day for only $3.50 a week.[13] He and his family worked all year long only to break even at the end of the year. Their debt at the local grocery store would be wiped clean and they would have to start off another year with no money saved. What the white man was doing was not fair. They expected him to shut up and be happy that they were robbing his family of the slight opportunity for them to get ahead. Loyd was not afraid of hard work, but he wanted something to show for it.

Sherman could remember his dad having a dream of owning his own business, whether it was a corner store, a juke joint, or any side job that would make the family a profit. Most people in the South had a side hustle. They sold wood, tomatoes, collard greens, or homemade preserves just to name a few. Loyd Byrd's store had never gotten off the ground. The nightclub dream was more of a nightmare and never materialized. One business venture seemed to be working: Loyd Byrd was good at making corn liquor. Financially, he had done a lot better selling corn liquor than he ever did picking cotton. People would trade food for liquor. Either way, food or money, Loyd made a profit. Unfortunately, Loyd's business venture landed him in jail on more than one occasion. [14] No matter how far back in the woods he would set up his production of corn liquor, the police eventually would sniff out the location. Because he was frequently absent, the matriarch Annie Lloyd was the mortar that held the Byrd family together. In spite of the pain and agony of his father's imprisonment, Sherman's love for both parents prompted him to step up and try to make a better life for himself and his mother.

Picking cotton in the fields of Carrollton had prepared Sherman and Butter Roll for the physical stresses of boot camp and beyond. Both young men were in excellent physical condition. That was the least of their problems. They were about to enter a cruel and vicious world without familial support. Annie Lloyd was not a naïve mother, and although Sherman and Butter Roll were about to get on the bus together, she knew the Navy eventually would separate them. As they continued to talk, Sherman and Butter Roll began to make their way to the open door of the bus, eager and determined.

Sherman could see his mother becoming tense. He and Butter Roll were two young colored men about to head across country on a white man's bus. It did not matter that they were traveling to enter military service. They still were expected to ride in the back. Negro men sometimes never reached their destination when traveling by bus in the South. Racist groups such as the Ku Klux Klan would overtake them at rest stops, torture and lynch them, merely for the color of their skin. [15] This reality did not deter them from launching out in hopes of a better life.

The bus was nearly filled to capacity. As the two young men approached the door, Annie's eyes locked in on the rear seats, as if to tell them, there are the seats where you sit. Although Sherman was a revolutionary in heart and mind, he would not break the written rule that said colored people were to sit in the back. Annie had nothing to worry about, at least from his perspective.

Sherman stepped onto the bus. He wanted to hug his mother before departing, but colored people were not allowed to show affection in public places. [16] Another one of those Jim Crow laws of etiquette they were required to observe. Such action, if ignored, could result in being arrested and placed in jail. Sherman was confident that everything would be all right. God was in the midst and He would take care of them. As Sherman made his way to the back of the bus, Butter Roll was right behind him.

After riding for about five hours, the bus stopped at a little diner in Holly Springs, Mississippi. It would only be a few more hours before they crossed the state line into Arkansas. The bus driver stood up and said "Everybody be quiet for a minute. I need to dish out some instructions. This is my usual stop on the way to the recruiting station. The owner and I have an agreement to fix your orders as quickly as possible so that I can get on down the road. Y'all niggers have to go around to the back door to order food and you can't use the diner's restroom. Y'all have to walk a little ways through the bushes in the back and there you will find an outhouse. Alright everybody back on the bus in an hour".

Sherman and Butter Roll scurried on off of the bus. The instructions did not seem unusual to them. Diners had the same rules in Greenwood, Mississippi. They decided to relieve themselves first and then go to the back door to order their food. As they opened the door to the outhouse, a swarm of flies flew out. They had to hold their breath as they entered for the smell was so bad. As they walked back toward the diner, Sherman turned to Butter Roll and cheerfully said, "Hey Cuz we are going to finally make it out of Mississippi!" Butter Roll laughed and answered, "Yep, but there were a few times when I didn't think we would!" No sooner than Butter Roll uttered the words out of his mouth, they saw five white men approaching them with sticks in their hands. Their eyes stretched wide open. They gazed at each other with fear. Sherman's heart began to race. It was beating so fast that he thought it might burst out of his chest. He could feel his shirt starting to stick to his back due to the large drops of sweat popping out all over. He could hear the words of his mother saying, "Never count your chickens before they hatch." He and Butter Roll were getting ready to celebrate their safe exit from the hatred filled state of Mississippi, but they were still a couple of hours away from the state line! It was now abundantly clear that they might not make it! Fight or flight? Neither option appeared good. They both froze in their tracks. Sherman thought to himself, was this a planned lynching, set up by the bus driver? A man with gray hair, a wrinkled face and a pot belly hollered out, "What are you niggers doing back yonder?" Butter Roll quickly answered, "Just came from the outhouse Sir. Our bus driver made a quick stop to grab something to eat. We are on our way to Little Rock, Arkansas to enlist in the United States Navy". The man replied, "Quit lying to me boy, the Navy don't enlist niggers!" A voice behind the old man sternly said, "Yes they do, and I aim to deliver every nigger placed in my care to the Navy Recruiting Station in one piece!" It was the bus driver!

Sherman had never been so happy to see a white man in his entire life! "You boys hurry on back to the bus now." Sherman and Butter Roll ran back to the bus making sure to go around the five men instead of running through the line which they had formed. As they sat down in their seats at the back of the bus, they could not stop trembling. Tears welled up in their eyes. Sherman looked over at Butter Roll and angrily said, "Let's make a promise to each other, right here, right now! We will do everything we can to make it in the Navy. We do not want our sons and daughters ever to experience the fear of being lynched! Oh God! Help us!" Butter Roll agreed, and they locked the pinky fingers of their right hands together, in that old familiar way. The same way they had done since they were five years old. Simultaneously they both said, "I promise!"

Three hours later they arrived at the main recruiting station in Little Rock, Arkansas.

This was where they would officially enlist. Sherman and Butter Roll exited the bus, and it did not take long for them to notice how segregation continued from state to state. All of the white recruits were examined first. The colored recruits had to wait at the back of the line.

As the examining surgeon rattled off Sherman's physical character-istics, he was baffled by the doctor's choice of words: five feet, eight-and-a-half inches tall; weight, 140 pounds; eyes negro, hair negro, complexion negro, color negro. Negro meant black or dark-skinned people. Butter Roll was described the same way: eyes negro, hair negro, complexion negro, color negro. It seemed as if white people would not even take the time to look at them. No effort was made to distinguish the difference between his appearance and that of his cousin Butter Roll. Butter Roll had brown eyes and a chestnut brown complexion. Sherman had dark brown eyes, with skin as black as night. Negro people would run to their homes whenever the police or town people were looking for a "nigger," who they thought committed a crime. They did not care much about the description as long as they found someone to capture. Mistaken identity was the demise of many colored men and women in the South. [17] Few white people were convicted in the court of law for this most heinous injustice.

Sherman and Butter Roll passed the surgeon's physical examination. Each of them was given a seven-digit service number. This became their new identities. They were instructed to memorize it before they stepped foot on the NTC in San Diego.

New recruits who were 17 years of age could only enlist for three years.[18] The only thing left to do was to sign on the dotted line. Sherman smiled to himself as he remembered the words of the Navy recruiter. The line was dotted. He had never signed a contract of any kind before. Contracts were new to him and he took the moment seriously. As a share-cropper he had learned that a man's word was his bond. They bartered and exchanged goods by giving their word that they would do a certain thing. A person's word was their money. Sherman signed on the dotted line. Then he bowed his head and asked God for the strength to honor his commitment.

His quest to fulfill God's purpose for his life steered him toward the anchor. The very essence of a chief was nestled in the fouled anchor. Was God calling him to be a chief? He could not see the whole picture, only a part. Hence, by faith, he began to move in that direction.

347 63 70   NAME **BYRD, Sherman (n)**   RATE $75.00

(SERVICE NO.)   (RATE)   (PAY PER MONTH)

DATE **27 December 1947**   **FIRST ENLISTMENT** ☒   **REENLISTMENT** ☐ **IN THE UNITED STATES NAVY**

(DAY) (MONTH) (YEAR)   FOR **THREE (3)** YEARS; MINORITY ☐

ACCEPTED AT **NRSS, GREENWOOD, MISS.** , ENLISTED AT **NAVCRUITSTA, LITTLE ROCK, ARK.**

OCCUPATION **Student**   **FFT to Recruit Training, NTS., San Diego, Calif.** CITIZENSHIP **U.S. NEGRO**

AGE OF BIRTH **Carrollton, Miss.**   DATE OF BIRTH **7 September 1930**   AGE **17** YRS. **03** MOS.

HOME ADDRESS **Rt. 1, Box 78**   **Greenwood**   **Leflore**   **Mississippi**

(STREET AND NUMBER) (TOWN) (COUNTY) (STATE)

NAME OF NEXT OF KIN OR LEGAL GUARDIAN **Loyd BYRD**   (RELATIONSHIP) **Father**

ADDRESS **Same as above**   MARRIED ☐ SINGLE ☒

CREDITED TO **3rd**   CONGRESSIONAL DISTRICT, STATE OF **MISSISSIPPI**

EDUCATION: GRADE SCHOOL **8** YRS.; HIGH SCHOOL **0** YRS.; COLLEGE **0** YRS.; POST GRAD. **0** YRS.

PREVIOUS SERVICE   IF NONE, CHECK HERE ☒

CONTINUOUS SERVICE CERTIFICATE NO. _____ — FIRST ENLISTED IN **REGULAR NAVY** ☐   **NAVAL RESERVE** ☐

DATE _____ PLACE _____ — LAST ENLISTMENT OR EXTENSION: REGULAR NAVY ☐   NAVAL RESERVE ☐

WITH _____ DISCHARGED AS _____ (RATE) WAS LAST DISCHARGED _____ (DATE) FROM _____

SERVICE IN REGULAR NAVY _____ (YEARS) (MONTHS) (DAYS)

NAVAL RESERVE _____ MARINE CORPS _____ COAST GUARD _____ ARMY _____

(YEARS) (MONTHS) (DAYS)   (YEARS) (MONTHS) (DAYS)   (YEARS) (MONTHS) (DAYS)

NATIONAL GUARD _____ (STATE) (DATE OF ENLISTMENT) (DATE OF DISCHARGE)

PHYSICAL CHARACTERISTICS

HEIGHT **5** FEET **6½** INCHES; WEIGHT **140** , EYES **negro** ; SEX **male** , HAIR **negro** ; COMPLEXION **negro** COLOR **negro**

(COLOR)

AT: **ANT: PM STOMACH; S3" STOMACH; PS R KNEE**

POST: PS BACK; S1" R ELBOW.

I CERTIFY that I have carefully examined, agreeably to the Regulations of the Navy, the above-named recruit, and find that, in my opinion, he is free from all bodily defects and mental infirmity which would, in any way, disqualify him from performing the duties of his rating, and that he has stated to me that he has no disease concealed or likely to be inherited.

_____ Examining Surgeon.

For and in consideration of the pay or wages due to me which may from time to time be assigned me during the continuance of my service, I agree to and with **C. E. ULRICH, Lt. (jg) USN, Asst. O.I.C.** of the United States Navy, as follows:

(NAME OF COMMANDING OFFICER)

First: To enter the service of the Navy of the United States and to report to such station or vessel of the Navy as I may be ordered to in, and to the utmost of my power and ability discharge my several services or duties and be in everything comfortable and obedient the several requirements and lawful commands of the officers who may be placed over me.

Second: I oblige and subject myself to serve { **3** years from **27 December** , **947** { during minority until. _____

unless sooner discharged by proper authority, and on the conditions provided by the act of Congress of March 3, 1875, as follows:

SEC. 1422. That it shall be the duty of the commanding officer of any fleet, squadron, or vessel arriving within an Atlantic or to a Pacific port of the United States [...]

In the event of war or National emergency declared by the President to exist during my term of service, I oblige and subject myself serve until six months after the end of the war or National emergency if so required by the Secretary of the Navy unless I voluntarily enlist or extend my enlistment. I understand that when so detained the addition of one-quarter pay as specified in Section 1422, Revised Statutes, is not applicable.

I also oblige myself, during such service, to comply with and be subject to such laws, regulations, and articles for the government of the Navy as are or shall be established by the Congress of the United States or other competent authority, and to submit to treatment for the prevention of smallpox, typhoid (typhoid prophylaxis), and to such other preventive measures as may be considered necessary by naval authorities.

Third: I am of the legal age to enlist; I have never deserted from the United States Navy, Army, Marine Corps, or Coast Guard; I have never been discharged from the United States Service or other service on account of disability or through sentence of either civil or military court; and I have never been discharged from any service, civil or military, except with good character and for the reasons given by me to the recruiting officer prior to enlistment. I am not a member of the Naval Reserve, Naval Militia, Marine Corps Reserve, National Guard, or Army Reserve.

Fourth: I understand that upon enlistment in the Naval Reserve, or upon transfer or assignment thereto, I may be ordered to active duty in time of war or when in the opinion of the President a National emergency exists, and that I may be required to perform active duty throughout the war or until the National emergency ceases to exist.

Fifth: I understand that if I become a candidate for the Naval Academy and fail to pass the entrance examination, I will be returned to general service.

Sixth: I have had this contract fully explained to me, I understand it, and certify that no promise of any kind has been made to me concerning assignment to duty, or promotion during my enlistment.

Oath of Allegiance: I, **Sherman (n) BYRD.**

do solemnly swear (or affirm) that I will bear true faith and allegiance to the United States of America; and that I will serve them honestly and faithfully against all their enemies whomsoever; and that I will obey the orders of the President of the United States and the orders of the officers appointed over me, according to the rules and articles for the government of the Navy.

And I do further swear (or affirm) that all statements made by me as now given in this record are correct.

Copy of Sherman Byrd's Enlistment Record
Courtesy of the United States Navy

CHAPTER TWO

CALL IT LIKE YOU SEE IT

With made-up minds and the determination to succeed, Sherman and Butter Roll set out for the NTC in San Diego. They knew that boot camp would be an uphill battle. Their goal was to graduate without ruffling too many feathers. They planned to follow orders as directed and learn as much as possible about becoming a skilled Seaman.

The community of San Diego welcomed the presence of Navy sailors. The Navy fueled a tremendous boost to the local economy. During World War II, hundreds of thousands of sailors passed through the NTC.[19] By the time Apprentice Seaman Byrd and Apprentice Seaman Brown arrived, the economy was slowing down.

The bus pulled into the NTC on December 30, 1947, at 9:00 in the morning, stopping at the front gate. On the left-hand side of the compound hung a huge sign that read, "Welcome Aboard. You are now men of the United States Navy. The Tradition of the Service Demands your Utmost Effort Give it Cheerfully and Willingly." [20]

Welcome to Boot Camp
Photo Courtesy of the United States Navy

There were those anchors again, one at the top left-hand corner of the sign and the other at the lower right-hand corner. Every time he saw those anchors he felt drawn to them. Like the song he often sang at church said, "We will understand it better by and by." God reveals things to his people in stages. It is similar to a person walking down a road on a foggy morning with just 20 feet of visibility. The farther he walks, the clearer the next 20 feet of the road becomes.

The words on the sign that said, "You are now men," held particular importance to Byrd. In the South, adult Negro men were called boys. If a man were 50 years old, white people would still call him "boy." They said it to emphasize their supposed superiority to colored people, no matter what age. "Come here boy!" "Fetch that boy!" The indignation embedded in the tone in which they said it was deplorable. They even allowed their children to call adult men "boy." It was beyond degrading. Jim Crow laws of etiquette did not allow white people to use courtesy titles of respect such as Mr., Mrs., Sir or Ma'am when referring to colored people.[21] Hatred and prejudices were taught behaviors. People were not born that way. White children were taught to be disrespectful—all they did was watch how their parents treated colored people and mimicked the same thing. This was not so in the colored communities. Children were taught to say, "Yes Ma'am and No Ma'am," or "Yes Sir and No Sir." It did not matter whether the person was colored or white; it was all about showing respect for their elders. Sherman had made up his mind a long time ago. He did not need anyone else's validation to determine whether he was a boy or a man. He was exactly who he thought he was: a young man determined to give his best efforts toward making the Navy his career.

Racism and hatred were not confined to the South but rather were widespread, even in the military. San Diego was almost 2,000 miles away but the prejudices were similar. For Byrd, the challenge was to graduate boot camp near the top of his class and without any altercations that would cause him to be kicked out. He braced himself for the onslaught of racial slurs and cruel deeds. His oldest brother Henry, who was in the Army, had warned him about certain things. His advice to his baby brother was this, "Find out what is required of you, and do it." [22]

Sherman knew that establishing a career in the Navy would require that he know what was expected of him at each stage of advancement, and then he would have to execute those requirements with precision. The armed forces consistently wrote down instructions indicating exactly how they wanted things done. Sherman wanted to remain focused on those instructions. He loved to read, so this fit well in his game plan. His plan was to read the instructions on how the Navy wanted things done. Then he would practice how to do it. He would also watch how the experienced sailors did it, and if he had any questions, ask the chief.

Sherman knew that he would have to pray his way through the negativity. He was prepared to use the weapon his mother had taught them to use a long time ago. It kept him for being harmed on more than one occasion. It was the weapon of his mind. Whenever he or his siblings found themselves in a confrontational situation with a white person, she encouraged them to remain calm and fight the battle in their mind. "They can't hear what you are thinking," she would say. "If they say, you are stupid, in your mind you say, I am smart! If they call you a nigger, in your mind you say, I am a child of God. Don't waste time fussing. You can show 'em, better than you can tell 'em. It is not what you say; it is what you do!" Annie Lloyd Keys Byrd was wise beyond her years, and he was glad that she was his mother.

Hard work earned his family respect from others. Most people respected hard workers, no matter what color they were. This survival technique was passed down from generation to generation. Annie Lloyd and her parents would have been beaten with a whip or killed for confronting a white person. Their mind was only one of the weapons they used in battle. Another weapon was prayer. Anytime, anywhere, any place, Sherman knew that he could call on the name of Jesus to help him in whatever situation he was facing. Years of using these techniques had paid off for Sherman. He believed the words he used in his silent battle, and it showed. Confidence exuberated from him like rays from the sun.

The Navy Buddy Program provided Sherman and Butter Roll with some degree of security. They knew how to look out for one another. They had been doing it all of their lives. Sherman was glad to know that he had Butter Roll by his side for at least 12 weeks. Where they went from there was anyone's guess.

The moment the doors of the bus opened, a six-foot, two-inch-tall man, with an immensely broad chest, bellowed out a barrage of curse words in a bone-chilling voice. The gist of what he said was that they all were a bunch of worthless turds, and it was his job to strip them of everything they thought they knew how to do and build them back up to do things the Navy way. The Navy way was the only way. The white people on the bus were ordered to line up on the right-hand side of the exit door, and the Negro people were to line up on the left. Each side was to form rows of five people across the front, with everyone else lined up behind them. He wanted them lined up by the time he counted to 20 and marched over to the Receiving Station by the time he got to 30. The recruits scrambled to get their belongings and hurried to exit the bus, bunching up at the door.

The man introduced himself as Chief Boatswain's Mate Robert Gray, the company commander. He informed them that they would be under his watchful eye for their designated weeks at boot camp. The Navy was segregated. There were white and Negro recruit units. Chief Gray proceeded to curse out all of them as he gave further instructions. Byrd was stunned; he had never experienced white people being belittled in the same manner as Negroes. Gray did not care if they were Negro or white. He wanted all the new recruits to know that he was in charge, and if they wanted to graduate from boot camp, they had better do exactly what he said, quickly and cheerfully. The sailor who accompanied Gray was Petty Officer First Class Howie Blunt, and it was his job to make sure each unit had their marching routines perfected before graduation day. Blunt instructed them to follow the foot movement of the person in front of them, and they marched over to the inventory room.

The sailors traded out their civilian clothes for their Navy uniforms. The Negro unit had to wait until the white unit had received their uniforms before approaching the counter. When Byrd stepped forward to retrieve his uniform, the second class petty officer threw it down onto the floor before Byrd even could get his hands on it. It was his way of saying that he was not pleased that Negroes were joining the Navy. What moved Byrd at that moment was not a sense of annoyance, but more so, expectance. He had been down this road before, and he knew how and when to get off the exit. Silence was the best killer, and Byrd had mastered the art. He picked up the uniform and proceeded toward the area designated. The petty officer could not read his thoughts. Byrd was thinking to himself; I am smart. I am calm. I can do this!

After about an hour of the recruits obtaining their necessary gear, they marched over to the base barber. Again, the white and Negro units had separate barbers. Recruits had to let go of their personal styles and fashions and conform to Navy standards. A clean- shaven appearance was part of the demeanor of a distinguished sailor.

The U.S. Navy had become a world leader thanks to their efforts to stop Soviet influence at the start of the Cold War. All eyes were on the Navy. It would only be logical for the Navy's service members to be polished in character and appearance. The Navy barber was there to ensure that every sailor's hair was in line with Navy standards. Any hair that was shoulder length would be clipped and dropped to the deck. The buzz haircut had more of an adverse effect on white people than Negroes. Byrd's hair was already cut low, and his chin was clean-shaven.

Most white people believed that Negroes were dirty and filthy, partly because of the high occurrence of disease among Negroes. They felt that it was disgusting to be touched by one of them. Byrd and Brown, however, were determined to show white people that their mindset was far from true. If Negroes had equal access to education, and medical treatment, the number of instances of disease would drastically drop.

They had many reasons to hope that white people's opinion of them would soon change. Rumors were floating about President Harry S. Truman moving closer to signing an executive order to end segregation in the armed forces. The writing was on the wall. From Byrd's vantage point, the Navy as well as the civilian population would have no choice but to accept the fact that Negroes could get the job done.

Byrd knew that the first task at hand was uniformity of appearance. Ever since Byrd was old enough to know how important appearances were, he had made a point to become a meticulous dresser. The teachers at Stone Street High School made sure that the young people paid strict attention to how they presented themselves. "Cleanliness was next to godliness," they often would say. Byrd's only sister, Ernestine had taught him how to wash clothes. Their clothes were not new, but they sure were clean. Cleaning clothes was one of the ways they often helped elderly family members. He and his brother Ned would stop by the home of elderly family members to chop wood, wash clothes, and weed out gardens. They did not have any extra money to give them, but they did have their health and strength, and they used it to help out in any way they could.

The three Navy barbers were dressed in what looked like lab jackets, not Navy standard- issued uniforms. As a sailor just coming into the military, Byrd was enamored by the idea that the Navy would have civilian barbers on base. Byrd and Brown walked to the back of the "Negroes-Only" line. Segregation was alive and real in the U.S. Navy. Their Negro unit had to stand in the back of the line for chow, physical exams, vaccination shots, and dental exams. Byrd and Brown made the best of their time together. They would laugh and joke with one another, and it seemed to make the time pass faster. One by one the barbers administered front-to-back swipes of the clippers to each of the recruit's head. The haircut had a lot to do with the recruits tossing aside their old identities and accepting the fact that they now were in the Navy. With hair now conformed to Navy standards, the unit marched over to the segregated barracks. Toilets, sinks, and water fountains were segregated too. Even a portion of the athletic field was sectioned off for Negroes only.

Civil rights and labor movement leader A. Phillip Randolph had already been hot on the tails of the Jim Crow philosophy. Byrd had read about Randolph and had grown to admire the work he had done for the cause of Negroes. After all, even in his case, Randolph's work was partly responsible for him being able to enlist. A. Phillip Randolph had the ability to influence policies of the federal government. In fact, Randolph had set the early stage for the eventual banning of segregation in the armed forces.[23]

Although it had not happened yet, Byrd could sense the tide starting to shift. Leaders in the civilian population had seen the big picture, rolled up their shirt sleeves, and begun to work to rewrite history. All humanity faced a common enemy and it required somebody with enough courage to stand against its oppressive character. Byrd saw Randolph as one of those heroes.

The first day on base, Byrd was ostracized, and so were the other Negroes in his unit. The majority of the white people had made it clear that they did not want to have any dealings with Negroes. Byrd grew up learning how to trust God because he had seen what trusting Him had done for his mother. His search for Jesus Christ had proven that the notion that Christianity was only for white people was false. Byrd understood that hatred was hatred. Deliberate and hateful actions toward Negroes did not line up with the teachings of Christianity. A man was right, or he was wrong. Byrd would not compromise his convictions of fairness and equity. He would rather stand-alone than to stand on the side of wrong.

Byrd understood that to receive respect; one had to give it. No matter the race, creed, or background, he was willing to treat every man equally. Determined to hold his ground, Byrd knew the importance of upholding his convictions at any cost.

The Negro unit was still in the early stages of its processing days, called P-days, so the company had yet to be declared fit for full duty. They read "the little talk" at the beginning of the Bluejacket's Manual, and it emphasized the paramount importance of obedience and good behavior. If a recruit would embrace obedience and perform at his highest potential, then he could reach the rate of a chief and possibly go on to be an officer. The Navy had a lot to offer.

Gray warned them about the reality, of the legality, of signing on the dotted line. They would face severe consequences for failing to honor their commitment to the Navy. It could result in loss of pay or possible jail time. [24] Byrd paid attention to the short talks Gray gave them. Obedience is better than sacrifice. As soon as the medical department cleared them for duty, rigorous physical training began.

White units went through eight weeks of boot camp. Negro units had 12 weeks of training. Even though Negros could read, they were labeled slow to comprehend. This presented a huge morale problem. Byrd did not feel that this was right. It was more a matter of a difference in exposure than comprehension. If someone had asked him to choose the vegetable out of a group of words such as apples, broccoli or potato, he would have chosen potato. He had never eaten broccoli before two days ago. Collard Greens, string beans, and cabbage were their vegetables. Almost every night, the Negroes in Byrd's unit would share the meanings of new words they had learned and the different things they had experienced. They were determined to make sure they all graduated from boot camp!

The Navy's Bluejacket's Manual was considered a type of Bible for new recruits. It contained information that all sailors should know such as the vessel's general characteristics. The recruits learned how to identify the ship, the forward (front end), midship (middle), and after (back end) parts, as well as how to pack a sea bag and administer first aid. They learned the correct way to swab (wash) a deck and paint a ship. [25]

Byrd was looking forward to the required swim test. It had been a while since he had been in the water. Swimming was his favorite sport. He was quite comfortable in the water. When he was young, his brothers would pick him up and see how far they could toss him into the Tallahatchie River. He would have to figure out how to swim his way back. Whenever he began to sink, they would faithfully jump into the river and save him. After retrieving him a couple of times and instructing him on what he was doing wrong, Byrd learned how to swim. Not only did he learn how to swim but he excelled at it, becoming an even faster and stronger swimmer than his brothers. God had blessed Byrd with a good set of lungs, and he could swim underwater for long periods of time. So much so that he often intentionally would scare his brothers by not coming up right away. They would dive frantically into the water in search of him. Then, he'd surface from underneath the water with a big grin on his face that totally exposed the gap in the middle of his two front teeth and a deep dimple on each cheek. Payback was common among brothers.[26]

The Negro unit could not swim in the same pool as the white unit. The denial of equal access to the swimming pool proved to be the biggest headache for company commanders during boot camp. Unique and creative alternatives often were employed. A separate pool was installed wherever possible, or they would complete the swim test down at the Young Men's Christian Association. The minimum requirements for classification of third class swimmers were to enter the water, feet first, from a minimum height of five feet, and swim 50 yards. Byrd successfully demonstrated the required techniques to qualify as a third class swimmer in the U.S. Navy.

Gray was impressed with Byrd's comfort level in the water. He glided through the water like a dolphin and was just as playful as one. Gray assessed Byrd's situation. This young man was only 17. It was likely that he would be the youngest person on the ship, no matter where he was assigned. Being the youngest person on the ship was similar to being the youngest of a bunch of older brothers. The other sailors would challenge him, telling him to go here, do this, don't do that. If he could keep a positive attitude, be humble enough to learn, and continue to use that youthful energy to his advantage, he could advance in the Navy. The Armed Forces was still not desegregated. Gray caught wind of it becoming a reality in a couple of months. Even with the law on his side, Gray knew that Byrd had an uphill battle to climb. He also knew, way down in his gut, that if any Negro could make it to CPO (E-7), the highest enlisted rate, it would be Byrd. Gray recommended that Byrd strike (be trained) for boatswain's mate. He had reviewed Byrd's records. Byrd scored well on his intake test, and he was a "take charge" kind of guy—a born leader who often volunteered to demonstrate the different techniques of seamanship tasks because he had practiced them until he could do it with perfection.

The boatswain's mate was one of the oldest ratings in the U.S. Navy, originating in 1794. Charged to care for the exterior of the ship, the boatswain's mate maintained equipment, handled cargo, ensured replenishment, and oversaw all small boats aboard the ship. One needed to be a jack-of-all-trades and hopefully Byrd would strive to master them all. Boatswain's mates are supervisors, planners, and schedulers. They are the deck crew foremen who plan and assign work. Once the work is completed, the boatswain's mate verifies compliance to operating procedures.

All areas of the ship that are not maintained by the engineering department comprise the boatswain's mate's responsibilities. He thoroughly inspects the vessel and performs routine; semiskilled; and skilled duties, such as cleaning, painting, and maintaining the vessel's hull.

Boatswain's mates are expert line handlers. They possess an extensive knowledge of knots, hitches, splices, and bends. They often work aloft. Effective communication skills are a must.

Deck crewmembers come from all walks of life and boatswain's mates must be able to converse with them all sufficiently.[27]

The Navy is full of tradition, and none as prominent as the boatswain's call using pipes (whistles of a sort) to make specific sounds to pass on information and orders. The general call is piped before an announcement and the still is used to call the crew to attention. Carry on dismisses the crew back to their duties, and call the boatswain's mate was piped to call the boatswain's mate. All pipes communicated some order or information to every sailor aboard.[28] Byrd certainly would make a great boatswain's mate, but Gray saw something else in him as well. As company commander, one of Gray's duties was to assess the recruit's current abilities and his future potential. After noting how natural it seemed for Byrd to be in the water and how long he could hold his breath before surfacing, Gray began to ponder an outrageous thought. Could Byrd one day become a Navy diver? The Navy was critically low on volunteers to train as divers.

One of the Jim Crow laws of etiquette did not allow white people and Negro people to swim together in the same public pools. Gray pondered, what in the world was he thinking? The future integration of the Navy was a big enough challenge for the moment. Executive Order 9981 was on the horizon. President Truman was on the cusp of integrating the U.S. Armed Forces and granting equal job opportunities for all. [29] Byrd would have his hands full just trying to deal with the integration of white and Negro sailors. He had no need to cloud his mind with anything else. Gray tossed to and fro while trying to sleep that night. His mind battled with the decision whether or not to tell Byrd about Navy divers. As a Navy chief, he was required to be a "straight shooter." He had to call things as he saw them. Although Byrd was already breaking through the norm by striking for an occupation other than a mess cook or porter, Gray saw something else besides deckhand in him. Byrd was smart, physically fit, and followed orders, he just was not white. Was the color of Byrd's skin enough to make him shrug off his responsibility as a chief? No, it was not. Gray settled the battle in his mind. He would talk to Byrd man to man, just like he did with the white recruits. Later that day, Gray stopped by the Negro barrack and told Byrd that he wanted to talk to him outside. Instructing him to come outside did not appear to be unusual. Company commanders seek out a time to talk to each recruit, usually for about 10 to 15 minutes each. Once alone, he explained to him that as his chief and company commander, he had made some observations. Byrd's ears perked up as he gazed down at Gray's feet.

Gray said, "I know this is your first time away from home. You are coming from an area where the notorious Ku Klux Klan was very active, but you are in the Navy now. Each day you arrive at the 9:15 morning inspection with a neatly worn uniform of the day. Your hair is properly cut, face cleanly shaven, and shoes spit shined. A lot can be determined by the way a man wears his uniform. You are authorized to wear a Navy uniform. From this point on, every man you encounter, white, Negro, Indian or Chinese, I want you to stand tall, look him straight in the eye, and say what you have to say. Toe to toe, man to man. Forget about those useless Jim Crow laws of etiquette. You are a U.S. Navy sailor, and you darn better act like one."

Byrd shuffled his feet, squared his shoulders, and looked Gray right dead in his eyes. It felt good. It felt really good, as if a weight had been lifted off of his shoulders. For ten years, he had been looking down at the ground as he conversed with white people. Not anymore. The invisible chains of the Jim Crow laws of etiquette were breaking one at a time.

Gray continued to share his assessment of how Byrd could best be an asset to the U.S. Navy. He explained to him how he felt that striking for boatswain's mate was a great fit for him. As a deckhand, Byrd occasionally would get to assist the Navy divers. Being the excellent swimmer that he was, this would give him the opportunity to see what Navy divers do, and decide whether he would like to volunteer to train for diving. The risk of injury and even death was high, but the fulfillment of a successfully completed mission was even higher.

Assessments are a vital part of the Navy's mission. Commissioned and noncommissioned officers are called upon to assess situations, people, places, and things. An accurate assessment can be the difference between success and failure, life or death. Gray gave Byrd a summary of his assessment of a way forward in his naval career. First, become a skilled seaman. Second, strike for boatswain's mate. Third, observe and assist the Navy divers, and consider the possibility of volunteering to become one. Finally, execute the things required to advance to E-7, boatswain's mate chief. If any of the other chiefs had heard the assessment he gave Byrd; they would have accused him of blowing smoke, giving false hope. Chief Gray was merely calling it like he saw it. He was content to leave the rest in God's hands.

CHAPTER THREE

THE GO-GETTERS

Byrd and Brown graduated from boot camp and advanced to Seaman Second on March 19, 1948. They were able to fly under the radar without getting into any major confrontations. Orders to their new duty stations required them to take separate paths, but they appreciated each other's support during boot camp. In April, the Navy transitioned into a new enlisted rating and warrant structure. Byrd and Brown's rating changed to Seaman Apprentice. Things around Byrd were changing at a lightning-fast pace; people were coming and going. The influx of new faces and situations continued day after day. One thing remained certain in this unpredictable environment. Wherever Byrd went or whatever he was assigned to do, a chief was waiting for him to report. Each and every enlisted sailor is passed from the watchful eye of one chief to another. Chiefs are challenged to instruct, demonstrate, and observe the execution of all assigned tasks. Professionals in their rating, chiefs are servant supervisors and are responsible for ensuring that the men receive food, housing, and training.

About the time Byrd graduated from the NTC, the Navy had introduced a new rating, the personnelman (PN).[30] Considering the rating was brand new, some may have thought it would be a promising rating for him to pursue, but not Byrd. No matter where he went integration was considered an experiment. He was a guinea pig under constant observation. Officers and enlisted personnel wondered are Negroes smart enough, strong enough, trustworthy enough, reliable enough? The list went on and on. Instead of whining about it, Byrd decided that he would do his best to represent Negroes as the smart, strong, trustworthy, and reliable men he knew them to be.

As a PN, Byrd would be an assistant to executive officers. It was an opportunity that many white people would walk over hot coals to fulfill. There would not be enough billets for every sailor who wanted to change ratings. He also would be an assistant for classification training, morale, welfare and the recruiting of officers. It was a great opportunity for sailors wishing to advance quickly.

Byrd knew that everything that shines is not gold. A man has to know the path that the Lord has instructed him to take and not be sidetracked by everything that glitters. Byrd would have none of that. He was a patient man, and he knew the value of waiting. Not only was Byrd extremely patient, but he was also strategic. Being a PN was not a part of his strategy. He understood why they wanted to steer him in that direction. It was because of his clerical test scores.

He scored high for a Negro who did not start school until the age of nine and only completed the eighth grade. Byrd scored 40 on his Armed Forces Qualification Test taken during the enlistment process. Further testing at boot camp yielded scores of General 40, Arithmetic 44, Mechanical 39, and Clerical 49.

His adversaries had nothing to worry about, at least in the area of personnel. Byrd was not the bureaucratic type, and he hated being caged in an office setting. He was a free spirit. He enjoyed two things the most: the outdoors and the water. Byrd remained focused on striking for boatswain's mate and was not interested in competing for PN.

As a young boy, Byrd had no other choice but to compete; he had three older brothers. He learned how to fight from his brothers, Henry, Albert, and Ned. A careful observer, he watched his brothers defend the family. Those experiences as a young boy taught him how to defend the important things in his life.

The competition between the boys in the Byrd family was intense. Even as a small child, Byrd was fiercely competitive and did not like to lose at anything. He developed an aggressive nature as early as the time when he played marbles against his brothers. During one summer, his brothers beat him in a pick-up game. The young Byrd did not take the loss lying down. After losing, he habitually went outside the house at night to practice his game, even in the dark, until soon he was able to beat his brothers. While others slept, Byrd practiced and continued to master his craft.

That same intensity he developed as a young child, he carried with him into the start of his naval career. In Byrd's mind, the idea of completeness didn't exist. He always had something else to learn. Byrd knew that for him to progress further in the Navy, he would need to be better than the majority of the other sailors. Negro men had to be twice as skilled as white men to warrant consideration for higher levels of responsibilities. A temporary assignment to the Flag Administrative Unit ComFair West Coast would develop his efficiency in the generation and documentation of paperwork. Boatswain's mates were responsible for maintaining various logs aboard the ship. Byrd resolved in his own heart not to turn down any opportunities to learn something new. PN was just not the direction the Lord was leading him to pursue.

After a brief two-week stint, Byrd transferred to USS *Tarawa* (CV 40), the Essex-class aircraft carrier. He was about to see the world. It was a huge leap from the cotton fields of Carrollton, Mississippi. Two months after he arrived on *Tarawa*, July 26, 1948, President Harry S. Truman signed

Executive Order 9981 establishing equality of treatment and opportunity in the U.S. Armed Forces.

On October 1, 1948, *Tarawa* deployed with Carrier Air Group One on a world tour escorted by Destroyers *USS Dennis J. Buckley* (DD–808), and *USS Hawkins* (DD–873). By October 10, 1948, the carrier had reached Pearl Harbor, Hawaii, and tied up to Ford Island, giving the crew a vivid view of the cloud-shrouded mountains of Oahu. The mountains were beautiful and picturesque. As the tugboats pulled the carrier closer, sailors gasped at the unmatched scenery of the island, absorbing the clear blue waters and the tallest of palm trees. It was a beautiful paradise. *Tarawa* was in port for a short stay and many of the sailors desired to go on sightseeing tours arranged by a local transportation company. There were so many sights to see. Some sailors took to the beaches of Waikiki just outside of the Royal Hawaiian Hotel, a sight that visitors seldom missed. [31] Byrd had another agenda. Deep down inside, Byrd was a man of initiative. He knew that a climb in rate would require extra efforts. It was a struggle that most of his white shipmates would never have to experience. Moreover, his growing awareness of the boatswain's mate rating began to give him more confidence. Byrd's increasing interest in being at the top of his class coincided with the fact that he wanted to make a career out of being in the Navy. He was a Carrollton boy that found a new home on floating pieces of steel. He had no intention of being anything other than a U.S. Navy sailor. It was the very reason he had enlisted. Because *Tarawa* was such a large carrier, Byrd had to work extremely hard to familiarize himself with it. He also knew however, that it was too much information to absorb all at once. He had to take one thing at a time.

For Byrd, the struggle to learn was twofold. As it was, the Boatswain's Mate Rate Training Manual was filled with an overwhelming amount of information, and he struggled to internalize it. What added to the drudgery was the denial of assistance from his shipmates. While on off-duty status, Byrd stayed on the ship to learn from on-duty personnel, but many refused to teach him. In their opinion, if he wanted to know about being the best Boatswain's Mate, he would have to learn on his own. Nothing had changed much since the end of the war. The tension felt by Negroes in World War II was the same tension Byrd now felt aboard *Tarawa*. They admired Byrd's effort but hated the color of his skin.

The day after *Tarawa* moored in Pearl Harbor; Byrd perused his Bluejackets manual and proceeded to work on his proficiency in marline-spike seamanship. According to the manual, he needed to perfect the art of knotting, splicing and seizing. [32] Byrd drafted a few ground rules for himself: he would not put down the manual or the lines until he had at least learned how to identify the components and characteristics of the different types of knots. Line-handling details were essential to the job of a boatswain's mate, and Byrd wanted to be an expert. Marlinespike sea-manship was dangerous, and if lines were not handled correctly, shipmates could die. Any loss of life would be a tragedy. In Byrd's mind, anything less than perfection was unacceptable. From the very start of his naval career, he became known for making sure things were done right. In the fleet, mis-takes were inevitable, but Byrd was determined to minimize them.

Being a young Negro in the Deep South prepared him for a life of cognizance and perception. Some of the sailors on the *Tarawa* could have sworn that Byrd had eyes in the back of his head. He was aware of his sur-roundings and he took notice of the smallest of details. This however, came with a price. Sailors who chose to be slackers hated Byrd and used every available opportunity to discredit him. To them, his efforts at perfection were loathsome. Nevertheless, Byrd quickly found out that his overall out-look in life would serve him well in the boatswain's mate rating. On his off time, Byrd practiced marlinespike seamanship for hours. Every ordinary seaman should know basic marlinespike work, such as knot a rope yarn, overhand knot, and figure-eight knot, just to name a few. The only way to learn marlinespike work was to practice the techniques. Byrd's outlook on perfection fit hand in hand with good seamanship. Practice was in his blood. He enjoyed the art of perfection and did not hesitate to put in the necessary work and time to obtain it. Byrd had learned to master that part of marlinespike seamanship before the *Tarawa* left the port of Pearl Harbor.

Byrd's zeal to learn did not go unnoticed. Although he was shunned by most of the white deckhands in his crew, he did not escape the watchful eye of Boatswain's Mate Chief Allen Stukes. The petty officers did not want to train Byrd because of the color of his skin. In their opinion, all he was good for was to be a runner, fetch this tool, bring me more paint, and clean out the scuttlebutts. Not wanting to rock the boat so shortly after arriving on the attack aircraft carrier, Byrd read as much as he could and watched the boatswain's mates work, observing their different techniques. Later during the day, while he was alone, he would practice what he saw.

Boatswain's Mate First Class Matthew Daniels stood near the gangway of the ship, where people came aboard or went ashore while in port. A group of four boatswain's mates and two enlisted men followed him everywhere he went. Daniels turned to the group and said, "OK men, listen up! I am going to go over the correct way to perform your duties as boatswain's mate of the watch while in port". Byrd's ears perked up as he stood within hearing distance about ten feet behind them. He moved in closer. Daniels saw him approaching the group and shouted, "Not you Seaman Byrd; no white man is going to take orders from a nigger! You cannot pass orders received from the officer of the deck, nor ensure that the side boys remain in their designated places on the ship. Furthermore, you cannot inspect the work of white sailors, nor arrest them for disorderly conduct! Who in their right mind allowed you to strike for boatswain's mate? Did they not know that you would be supervising white men"? Byrd shuffled his feet, squared his shoulders, and looked Daniels directly in his eyes, just as Chief Gray from boot camp instructed him to do. "No disrespect intended Boats, but anything they can do, I can do. All I need is the same training and a chance to show you I can", said Byrd. "Not in this lifetime!" said Daniels as the sailors who were being trained turned towards Byrd shouting out obscenities.

"That's enough!" shouted Stukes, who overheard the conversation as he was about to go ashore. "I will not tolerate any one's refusal to train a fellow boatswain's mate. The very essence of our rating embodies on-the-job-training. To deny a Seaman an opportunity to learn the skills that will allow him to advance in rate is unacceptable. The safety of every sailor aboard this ship is predicated on the boatswain's mate's knowledge and skills. I hereby dismiss weekend liberty until all Seaman aboard this ship have acquired the necessary skills to advance to boatswain's mate third class!" Stukes was furious! He did an about face and shouted for Daniels to follow him. The other boatswain's mates walked away in frustration.

Stukes quickly reeled in their behavior. They adversely affected the proper flow of the training process. As a chief, he could not go soft on his sailors. He must call a spade a spade. He refused to tolerate their prejudices for it resulted in a breach of their responsibilities. A chief must maintain control of his crew at all times.

Stukes reprimanded each boatswain's mate involved, beginning with Daniels for he was in training to be a chief. As the leading petty officer of the deck crew, it was his responsibility to teach those sailors junior to him by example. After that, everybody and his brother tried to share their knowledge with Byrd. They may not have shared it with a smile, but nevertheless, they did share.

Training would not be compromised. It was a matter of life or death in so many of the boatswain's mates' duties. Stukes did not consider himself to be a so-called nigger lover. He was a chief. He was clear on the orders he received from his commanding officer. No matter how unpleasant the orders may be, they must be executed. It was his job to transition his crew from disobedience to obedience, by any means necessary.

Byrd was like a sponge. He bounced around that aircraft carrier like a kid in a candy store, learning as much as he could wherever possible. His youthful energy was a definite plus to those with whom he worked. It did not take them long to realize that they could share their knowledge with Byrd and still use him as a runner. Byrd was a quick learner, and those youthful legs seemed to never stop moving. The boatswain's mates intentionally kept him busy.

So it was that day when Byrd first had the opportunity to watch as the boatswain's mates assisted a team of Navy deep sea divers. Their diving rig had pulled up on the starboard side of the ship. There was a slow seeping leak in the side shell plating of the engine room. The divers were there to locate, isolate, and monitor repairs. Intrigued by the professionalism of their demeanor and the respect given them by the sailors aboard, Byrd's interest peaked. He remembered the suggested career path his boot camp company commander had suggested. Dare he dream to become a boatswain's mate chief and a Navy diver? The thoughts running through his head were too much for him to absorb right then. From the cotton fields of Carrollton, Mississippi, to the highest enlisted rate in the U.S. Navy would be a feat in itself. Byrd sat down in hopes of slowing down his fast beating heart. He calmed himself by concluding that it was not a decision that had to be made right away. He promised himself to do some research on Navy divers and make a decision at a later date. He was interested, but his focus was on learning as much as he could to advance to Seaman.

Byrd had been on *Tarawa* for less than a year and already was showing signs of being a squared-away sailor. He received a Letter of Commendation from the Commander, U.S. Naval Forces Eastern Atlantic and Mediterranean, Admiral Ryan M. Copperfield. On January 17, 1949, His Royal Highness, Prince Manuel, Minister of Defense, Saudi, Arabia, American Minister K. W. Chart, and their official parties were guests of officers and men of the ship. Air operations, strafing attacks by aircraft on towed spar, 20-40 MM firing at towed sleeve, and a refueling of USS Hawkins (DDR-873) were conducted. Admiral Copperfield stated, "Such actions on the part of your Navy may repay our Country many-fold benefits. Well done to you and your men."

Stukes encouraged the steady advancement of all the petty officers and seaman in his crew. To advance, the sailors had to demonstrate that they possessed the knowledge and skill to perform certain tasks while in a wartime situation adequately. It was the responsibility of the chief to ensure that each sailor under his supervision, E-1 through E-6, would be ready when called.

The role of a CPO was much larger than the sailor who occupied it. His leadership would be measured by how well the men who followed him obeyed instruction. If the sailors in his crew were not advancing in rate, this echoed poor supervision. Stukes made sure that the nonrated men served productive apprenticeships in their rating. He outlined a path of applicable courses of study for Byrd to be advanced. Stukes did not micromanage Byrd but verified that he was studying. [33] Those who had paid attention knew that Byrd was a rate climber, even if they did not like him much for his efforts. On April 18, 1949, after 11 months of sea duty, Byrd transferred from *Tarawa* to Commander Charleston Group, Atlantic Reserve Fleet, U.S. Naval Base Charleston, South Carolina for duty aboard *USS Arcadia* (AD 21).

Byrd maintained his focus at a time when Negroes were considered to be at the bottom of the sociological barrel. He was one of the youngest crewmembers on *Arcadia*, a Klondike-class destroyer tender. At first, he was uncomfortable with that reality, but he quickly learned to employ his youth as an advantage. At every opportunity, he would listen and internalize the knowledge of the senior enlisted sailors. As he worked in his rate, Byrd frequently paid attention to scuttlebutt chatter and tactical strategies. He was careful, however, not to let on that he was listening in on conversations because he knew they did not particularly wish to share knowledge with him. Byrd kept his ears open, and his eyes forward, because he understood he was a constant and painful reminder of Negro infiltration.

Byrd's days were filled with manual labor, heavy lifting, and the swabbing of decks. He stayed busy. While he worked to maintain the exterior of the ship, the four other Negroes on the ship worked in the galley as mess cooks. They would meet up at the end of the workday and talk about where to go to relax.

Sherman Byrd – the early years
Photo Courtesy of the Byrd Family

Boatswain's Mate Chief David Goodman knew that approximately 10 percent of the men under his supervision were "self-starters." The other 90 percent were content being average sailors, doing what they were told, not showing much initiative.[34] He initially expected Byrd to fall in that category. To his surprise, Goodman soon found out that Byrd was marching to a different drumbeat. He was not aboard to conform to anyone's, much less Goodman's, predetermined statistics. It was evident Byrd was on a mission to be an above-average boatswain's mate and chief. On October 16, 1949, Byrd advanced to Seaman.

CHAPTER FOUR

EYES FOR A SAILOR

The Charleston Naval Base, originally known as the Navy Yard, was located six miles north of where the Ashley and Cooper Rivers meet to flow into the Atlantic Ocean. It sat on the west bank of the Cooper River. Before its construction, the city of Charleston was a fiscal disaster, primarily because of the effects of the Civil War. Although the War had economically decimated the Charleston area, the U.S. Navy, in accord with the 56th Congress, granted the city the contract to build the yard in 1890.

The Navy took possession of the property in 1901. Since its formation, the Charleston Naval Base had a tremendous impact on the local community, the Tri-County Area, and the entire state of South Carolina. The base showed tremendous growth until the onset of the Great Depression, which hit Charleston with full force between 1922 and 1932. During this decade, the Navy considered closing the base on three different occasions because of an extreme lack of work.

Just as the Great Depression was about to gain more momentum, however, the Charleston Naval Base received a shot in the arm in 1933. The base was designated as a new construction yard, which would create greater facilities and a larger workforce.[35] As it was being built in 1933, it foreshadowed a personal connection years in the making between two love-struck people—a Navy sailor and a teenage girl.

The same year the naval base got an extension on its lifespan, a baby girl was born to Mr. and Mrs. James and Irene Arnold. Her name was Louise, affectionately known as Weez. She had a brother, James Arnold Jr., who was four years older. He liked to be called Arnold. In the early years of her childhood, Weez learned the harsh reality of accountability and hard work. She was practically thrown into the life of an adult child. World War II was the culprit. Her father James had received "The Card," an official draft notification and went off to the Army. Her mother had to work to keep a roof over their head and food in their mouths. This left it up to Weez to keep the household going. At the tender age of nine, Weez was cooking, cleaning, washing, and ironing clothes. Her mother Irene worked at the hospital as an orderly on the night shift. Irene would be home by morning to see Arnold and Weez off to school. Sometimes at night, Weez would be afraid. Her brother Arnold would assure her that everything was going to be all right. He was the man of the house and at age 13, he was well capable of protecting her. Weez's father and mother never had the opportunity to attend school.

They could not read or write. Irene was determined that Arnold and Weez would not fall into that same misfortune. She made sure they attended school. Receiving letters with money from their dad was few and far in between. So, Weez took care of all of the household chores while her mother brought home whatever money she could to sustain them. Weez found little time for the recreation that most kids her age enjoyed. There was not much time for developing friendships either. It was not until her mid-teens that Weez began to draw a host of friends, mostly female.

Louise Arnold Byrd
Photo Courtesy of the Byrd Family

In November 1949, Navy ships were moored to the pier on Columbus Street in Charleston, and Weez's family did not live too far from the naval base. Sailors often were found in the general vicinity. One of them was Sherman Byrd.

Weez's brother Arnold was in the Navy. He and Sherman were not on the same ship, but they had met casually in passing at the naval base. They had become good friends. Arnold mentioned to Sherman that their landlord had a room for rent. Sherman was glad that he mentioned it. He rented the room. This gave him something to look forward to at the end of the workday. Separating work from the place he would call home went a long way toward helping him relieve stress. Getting a reprieve from the blatant racial discrimination on the ship was very much needed.

Sherman walked up to the house located at 48 South Street. It was a two-story home with a gray stone slab front and a three-step porch with a stoop for sitting. The steps led to a long porch that ran half the length of the house on the left-hand side. At the end of the porch was a door that led to the kitchen. The kitchen had a window that peered out to the walkway. The walkway led to a backyard that had another rectangular-shaped building with a bathroom, dining room, and large bedroom. The dining room was furnished with a table and four chairs. Two sets of bunk beds were in the bedroom. Mr. Theodore and Diane Ford owned the home. They lived upstairs and rented out the downstairs and the detached dorm-style room in the back yard for extra money.

One of the best things about retreating to this rectangular room called home was accessing it. As Sherman walked through to the back yard, he would be greeted by the smell of collard greens, lima beans, and fresh rolls. It reminded him of his mother's home cooking, and he welcomed every sniff. He would look up at the window in the kitchen and wave to the teenage girl eagerly peering out. Sixteen or 17 years old he guessed, for he knew she was still in high school. Sherman was 19 years old.

Her name was Weez, and she lived in the downstairs portion of the home with her mother and stepfather Thomas White. Her father James's infidelity had caused her parents to split. They both remarried and remained friends for the sake of the children. They lived two blocks apart.

Sherman often would stop and chat with Mr. Thomas as he sat on the stoop of the porch in the evening. Mr. Thomas drove a long-distance truck and enjoyed telling Sherman about the different routes he had driven and the things he had seen. The conversation would end with Mr. Thomas inviting him in to have a bowl of black-eyed peas, rice, and ham hocks,

"Hopping John," as Southerners called it. Now that was some good eating. Sherman would sit at the kitchen table with both hands firmly placed on top of it in anticipation. The four fingers on each hand would be tightly curled inward toward his body, and both thumbs would be pointing straight up in the air. Then he would break out in a little dance while still seated in the chair! Doing a dance called the two-step! His body and feet would move one step to the left and then to the right. Sherman loved to eat, and southern food was his favorite!

Sherman remembered the first day that he saw Weez from more than the chin up. Goose bumps went up and down his arms. She was a pretty little thing, all five feet, three inches of her. Weez Arnold was warm and inviting. Her beautiful dark brown skin was smooth and without blemish. People were drawn to her captivating smile. Always eager to meet new people and to lend a helping hand, she knew no strangers. Weez knew how to take charge. She was the one who could bring order to chaos. Slightly bow-legged like her dad James, Weez was always moving. Every time Sherman saw her she was cooking, washing clothes, or cleaning up something around the house. She also cared for her four younger siblings, two sisters and two brothers. Now and then, Weez would be called upon to babysit her five siblings from her father James Arnold Sr.'s union with the neighbor down the street, four sisters, and one brother. She also had an older brother, Thomas White's son, who lived in New York with his mother. All in all, Weez had eleven siblings. She loved children and found joy in caring for them, despite all the work. Weez was the personification of Southern hospitality, and Sherman had not visited any other city as hospitable as Charleston, South Carolina. Her smile lit up the room. She was the boss of the kitchen, telling her siblings to go and wash their hands and pointing out where they should sit—all the while opening and closing the lids on different pots on the stove. Sherman could tell she had years of experience cooking. Weez rarely sat down. He admired how she ran the household. Now and then their eyes would lock, and he hoped that she was interested in getting to know him better. He was interested in getting to know her. First, he would have to get permission from Mr. Thomas to ask her out.

Mr. Thomas said, yes, and Sherman and Weez spent the next Saturday at Mosquito Beach. Things clicked for them from the start. Sherman was the quiet type, and Weez was the life of the party. The rhythm and blues song, titled The Huckle-Buck, by Paul Williams began to play on the jukebox.[36] Louise shouted, "That's my song!" as she pulled Sherman up to dance. "Ah shucks now!" said Sherman, as he started dancing with Weez. Even when he danced, Sherman would hold his hands up near his waist, with the two thumbs sticking straight up in the air. Weez would smile every time she saw it. That was his signature move; no one else did that but him. Weez was happy! The two of them were getting along well. She smiled, he smiled.

Sherman used to feel self-conscious about the gap between his two front teeth. When he was a child, the neighborhood kids would call him "snagga tooth." He conditioned himself to keep his mouth closed in the hopes that the name-calling would stop. One day his sister Ernestine brought something to his attention. Only the boys were calling him names. All that the girls seemed to notice when he smiled were those beautiful dimples. Not many people had two deep dimples like he did. By the age of 12 years old, Sherman no longer cared what the boys said anymore. He smiled every chance he got. His dimples were stunning, and women of all ages were not shy about telling him so.

Sherman felt comfortable around Weez. They would talk for hours at a time, and their conversations never were boring. He felt that they were meant to be together. They laughed at the same things. They courted steadily for six months, and each time the ship would depart for a while and then return, Sherman would teach Weez the latest dances from other parts of the country. Dances like the cha-cha-cha.[37] It was his favorite move, and he could do it well. Sherman missed Weez whenever he was away. He was contemplating asking for her hand in marriage.

Sherman was a fan of reading instructions when it came to learning something new. However, he could find no clear guidelines on how to know when the woman you loved was the one to be your wife. Sherman listed on a piece of paper the pros and cons of marrying Weez. The pros outweighed the cons. Sherman waited for the opportunity to come when he would be able to talk to Mr. Thomas alone as he sat on the stoop of the front porch. He eagerly watched for him as he returned each day from the ship. Three days passed and there was no sighting of Mr. Thomas. As Sherman walked toward 48 South Street on the fourth day, he could see Mr. Thomas sitting on the stoop of the porch from a block away. His stomach began to knot up as he rehearsed the words in his mind. "Mr. Thomas, how are you doing today Sir?" Sherman asked as he sat down on one of the steps of the porch. "Good, how about you?" Mr. Thomas answered. "I am ok, Mr. Thomas, but I could be doing much better. May I ask Weez for her hand in marriage?" asked Sherman. Mr. Thomas's eyes opened wide as he blurted out, "Is she pregnant?" "No, no, no, Mr. Thomas, Weez is not pregnant. I love her very much Sir, and I want her to be my wife." Mr. Thomas took a sigh of relief and told Sherman to come into the house and join him for a drink. They needed to talk about some things before he could give him an answer. Sherman said he would be glad to come in, but he did not want to join him for a drink. The two of them talked well into the night before Mr. Thomas finally granted Sherman permission to ask Weez for her hand in marriage. Sherman proposed to Weez the following day. Weez said, yes, and a month later on June 6, 1950, they were married. Her parents loved Sherman like a son and gladly accepted him into the family.

THE KOREAN WAR

Byrd returned to *Arcadia* from a five-day leave period. Marrying Weez was the best decision he ever made. Just a few weeks after he returned to work from his honeymoon, the Korean War began. North Korea invaded South Korea with roughly 75,000 troops. The 38th parallel, an agreed-upon boundary marker between the two countries had been crossed violently on June 25, 1950. American troops did not enter the fight on behalf of South Korea until a few weeks later.[38]

At about the time the war started, Byrd's enlistment was scheduled to expire. The first two years of his enlistment had been extremely challenging. Now he was coming up on its third year, and he had a critical decision to make. Many asked the question, would he reenlist? Three years usually were enough to know whether or not blue shirts would extend their naval careers. Upon expiration, sailors who did not adapt to military life well or bleed navy blue and gold could take their walking papers and head back to life as a civilian. Navy blue and gold were the official colors of the Navy. The color navy blue represented the oceans and seas, and the color gold stood for integrity and valor.[39] War was usually the strongest deterrent of reenlistments.

The Korean War continued to gain steam with no guarantees that it would be a temporary conflict. World War II lasted nearly half a decade, and now America was engaged in another war, only this time it was Communism, not Nazism. The economic collapse and the political instability caused by World War I led to the rise of fascism in Europe. The Allies were fighting fascist world domination in World War II. This made resolution of the Korean War conflict extremely urgent. No relief was in sight. Byrd had many questions on his mind about the conflict. Should he remain in the Navy and fight to protect the interest and security of a country that hated the color of his skin? Should the United States become involved in resolving a civil war between people of the same nationality with different political views? Shouldn't the United States be more focused on its civil war between Negroes and white people?

Byrd wondered: What about this fight benefited Negro people? What about this fight benefited America? The benefit to America was the protection of its borders against Communist influence. In April 1950, a National

Security Council report known as NSC- 68 had recommended that the United States use military force to "contain" Communist expansionism anywhere it seemed to be occurring, "regardless of the intrinsic strategic or economic value of the lands in question."[40]

One of the benefits to Negroes was that it was another opportunity to break the chains of discrimination. Byrd wholeheartedly agreed with the core beliefs of the "Double V campaign". A campaign which was so fervently executed by the Pittsburgh Courier, a Negro newspaper distributed on a weekly basis. The Courier stated, "We, as colored Americans are determined to protect our country, our form of government and the freedoms which we cherish for ourselves and the rest of the world, therefore we have adopted the Double V war cry--victory over our enemies at home and victory over our enemies on the battlefields abroad. Thus in our fight for freedom we wage a two-pronged attack against our enslavers at home and those abroad who will enslave us. WE HAVE A STAKE IN THIS FIGHT... WE ARE AMERICANS, TOO!" [41]

Given that Byrd was assigned to *Arcadia*, the likelihood of his setting foot on Korean soil was zero to none. The war did not serve as a threat to Byrd's life. If his mission called for him to put "boots on the ground," he would comply without hesitation. Before joining the military, Byrd had made the decision to make a career of his service in the U.S. Navy. He was aware of the likelihood that his career years could include war and conflict. Byrd honored his commitment. He was in for the long haul.

Since his youth, Byrd had been a fighter. The fact that he made it three years in a racist Navy was a clear sign to him that he could face any challenge on the battlefield. No matter what the cost, the Korean War did not scare Byrd into signing discharge papers.

Officers aboard *Arcadia* had no choice but to be impressed with Byrd's focus. He thoroughly familiarized himself with the Boatswain's Mate Rate Training Manual. In the heat of racial tension, Byrd showed that he could lead a group of sailors, white and Negro, and do it with professionalism. The war did not distract him from accomplishing satisfactory completion of the Navy Training Course and Practical Factors for BM3 with a mark of 3.2. Byrd scored a 3.6 on the Navy Training Course for Petty Officers. Some argued the war fueled his energy.

Chief Goodman took these high scores into consideration during his quarterly assessment of Byrd and evaluated his proficiency in rate, seamanship, and conduct. He then forwarded the recommendation marks to his superior officer. The officer reviewed the chief's recommendations and generated the mark, a performance evaluation on a scale between 0.0 (the lowest) and 4.0 (the highest). The officer normally accepts the chief's recommendations. Lieutenant Junior Grade Dustin Hamilton recommended Byrd for reenlistment for several reasons, his high score on the BM3 exam, a mark of 3.9 in seamanship, and good conduct.[42]

The Navy reenlistment process required the generation of a new contract. A sailor would have to be discharged from his previous commitment and then recommit for a new period. If the sailor departed on good terms, the discharge would be deemed honorable. If he departed on bad terms, the sailor would receive a dishonorable discharge. Byrd was discharged at Charleston, South Carolina with an Honorable Discharge. He was now 20 years old, five feet, nine inches tall. Consistent weight lifting and exercise strengthened him, and his weight increased to 160 pounds. Byrd received $292.78 for 57 days of unused leave, travel expenses back to Greenwood, Mississippi, and a reenlistment bonus of $360.00. Some people recognized he was a change agent. He frequently manifested his ability to create positive change. Byrd also understood that if any further change was to occur in military race relations, someone had to step up and make it happen. Why not him? He was only one sailor, but his ability to see the big picture gave him the courage to be an example for the many young Negro men who someday would follow.

On December 27, 1950, at the recommendation of his commanding officer, Byrd reenlisted into the Navy for six more years. He was also recommended to receive a Good Conduct Medal. The Good Conduct Medal meant a lot to Byrd. It was a major accomplishment, particularly in light of the racism he had to endure. Negroes in America, especially in the military, were expected to remain passive and to accept whatever white America handed them. Fortunately, plenty of civil rights leaders, President Harry S. Truman, and the Fahy Committee (a seven-member panel focusing on equality in the armed forces) did not subscribe to the same philosophy. Negroes were a valued entity in the Korean War. Desegregation became a strong necessity. During the Korean War, shortages of white manpower demanded that the military work toward solidifying integration.[43] Desegregation accelerated further when commissioned officers learned that it improved morale among Negroes without causing racial friction, an idea that many in the "whitewashed" military feared.

In Byrd's mind, there was no better time in the history of the military for Negroes to advance than at the start of the Korean War. Communism was certainly worth fighting against, and America was hard pressed to get involved and to prevent it from spreading further around the globe.

Byrd recognized the importance of keeping in line with his commander-in-chief. Insubordination was a death sentence to a military career, especially for Negroes. As he continued to monitor the war from *Arcadia*, it became obvious that General Douglas MacArthur was rubbing Washington the wrong way. The general's insubordination did not sit well with the Truman administration. On April 11, 1951, in a dramatic and controversial gesture, President Truman dismissed General MacArthur from his military command. [44]

When word hit *Arcadia*, the reaction to MacArthur's firing was diverse: some agreed and others disagreed. Some thought that Truman had overextended his reach.

Regardless of how he might have felt, it was career suicide for Byrd to show any resistance or aggression toward the upper chain of command. The three years he spent in the Navy taught him how to remain neutral in certain circumstances. In Byrd's mind, Truman's decision to fire an insubordinate Army general was one of those circumstances. Whether or not he agreed with the decision, it was not his call to make; and as a sailor in the Navy, he was responsible for complying.

Truman's replacement for General MacArthur in Korea was General Matthew Ridgway. When the news media asked General Ridgway about his thoughts on segregation of the military, he replied, "I think segregation is both un-American and un-Christian." General Ridgway utilized integrated troops in the Korean War and successfully pushed the Soviet-backed North Koreans to the 38th parallel. Negroes proved they could execute strategic plans with skill and ability equal to white troops. The success of the integrated "boots on the ground" in the Korean War did a lot to further the equal rights of Negroes in all branches of the military. [45]

CHAPTER FIVE

THE APPLE DON'T FALL FAR FROM THE TREE

Racism in the military was not the only threat that Sherman had faced. In fighting those uphill battles, he often thought of his mother and some of the stories she shared with him. From his early childhood, it seemed that Sherman's life would be filled with threats and perils. Some of his experiences as a child seemed to be nothing more than preparation for a life of hazards. No one knew that more than his mother, Annie Lloyd Byrd.

She often reminded him of the day the Lord spared his life. She knew her son was destined to do great things, for he had tapped death on the head and lived. When Sherman was two years old, Annie Lloyd was in the field hoeing up weeds. It was a normal hot, sunny day, September 10, 1932. The date was forever etched in her mind. Sherman sat down on an old, empty, burlap potato sack, tied to a rope on one end, and fitly wrapped around her waist at the other. Close enough for her to observe if he was putting any odd things in his mouth, but far enough away, not to impede her motion. It was a timed reaction. Her eyes would peer up in his direction every so many seconds.

Her bent-over frame casually would sway to the right, peek at him, and sway back to the left in a dancing motion. Thousands of uneventful sways did not deter her from repeating it over and over again. Mothers develop routines that will bring them peace and assurance that their child is safe. Some routines may be longer in time or shorter, depending on the child. Sherman was an active child, inquisitive and strong. A quick learner with the deepest dimples she had ever seen. Yes, two of them, one on each cheek that gave way to a wide and heart melting smile. His black skin glistened with sweat under the mid-afternoon sun. He knew how to busy himself, clutching the toy she had made for him out of some leftover material from a bag of flour. She had placed several smooth stones inside the bag and tied it tightly together at the top. There were just enough stones in the bag to make a little noise. The stones had multiple shapes to satisfy his need to feel something different. Sherman was a happy child.

Nothing could have prepared Annie Lloyd for that one bodily sway and watchful eye that did not bring peace, but panic. Her eyes beheld something so terrible that her whole body froze. Horrible thoughts ricocheted through her mind incapacitating her ability to focus on the crisis at hand. Her bouncing baby boy was reaching his chubby right hand out toward the side of the burlap potato sack to pet a rattlesnake on the top of the head. Sherman gently tapped the snake as if it were a new-found toy.

On a breezeless day, God sent a breeze. It kept her from fainting. Annie Lloyd blinked.

The salt from the sweat of the noon-day heat, stung as it entered her eyes. She dared not wipe her brow. Her son's life depended on her every motion. Silently, she shouted, "Jesus" with all her might! Her mother Mary Alice always told her that a time would come in her life when she would not be able to say a long prayer. She encouraged her daughter to live a lifestyle of obedience and closeness to God so that when the moment came when there was no time to pray, He would answer before she called. Calling on his name freed her mind, heart, and body from the bondage of fear that had paralyzed her. She gathered her thoughts. Annie Lloyd knew her chances. She had but one shot, one swing, to save her son from the painful death of a rattlesnake bite. The head of the rattler had risen up off of the ground in attack mode. She had no money, nor shoulder of ham to use for payment to a doctor. Even if she ran, Sherman would not survive the three-mile trip. Sometimes you don't know that God is all you need until God is all you have. She stood straight up and stiffly took two steps to the right to face her enemy. She heard the rattling of his tail. It did sound like a toy! She raised her hand. Sherman raised his hand. She swiftly brought down the hoe on the snake, chopping it in half. The front half of the snake continued to move. She struck it on the head with the second swing. The corner of the hoe nicked Sherman's right knee, for he sat in that familiar way that babies sit, legs bent at the knees in the shape of triangles. Annie Lloyd fell to her knees. Trembling, she picked up her son and held him tightly. He had escaped being bitten by a poisonous snake, but whether he would survive the tight squeeze from his mother was questionable. He cried. She cried. The bright red blood from the gash in his knee stained her dress. She wiped Sherman's knee with her dress, hoping to get a closer look at the depth of the gash. It was the most beautiful gash that she ever had seen. Her son was alive!

Words of praise filled her mouth: "Thank you, Jesus! Thank you, Jesus!"

She had been wrong about her chances. God had given her two chances to kill that snake, and she was able to deliver a fatal blow to the head. With tears still flowing down her cheek, the words that her mother Mary Alice often said to her rung loud and clear in her heart, "Not only is He a God of a second chance; He is the God of another chance!" [46]

Every time Sherman thought of his mother's story, it gave him the shivers. He recognized that God had spared his life. Surviving the ordeal made him realize that his life had purpose and meaning. No one else on *Arcadia*, however, would have agreed that his purpose in life was to be a chief petty officer in the U.S. Navy.

Annie Lloyd Keys Byrd
Photo Courtesy of the Byrd Family

BM3 BYRD

The apple don't fall far from the tree. Byrd was familiar with this old saying frequently used in his hometown of Carrollton, Mississippi. It meant that children shared a lot of the same character traits and behaviors as their parents. Sherman added a new twist to the adage. The same thing was true about a chief and his petty officers. If a petty officer wore a sloppy uniform, pants dragging the ground, and anything less than a perfect cube in his neckerchief, this reflected poorly on his chief. Byrd would not make that mistake.

On April 16, 1951, he advanced to boatswain's mate third class (BM3). Few things felt better than donning the uniform of a third class petty officer in the U.S. Navy. When it came to dressing out, Byrd made it his personal mission to receive the highest possible score of 4.0. Now that he had been promoted to the rate of petty officer, his approach would not change. In fact, he purposely worked even harder on presenting himself as a bona fide military professional.

Less than a month after donning the eagle, the cross-anchors, and the chevron, Byrd took leave from his duty station and traveled to Carrollton, Mississippi. It was May 10, 1951. The bus ride from Charleston, South Carolina, was more than 670 miles west.

Byrd's return home as a third class petty officer was met with mixed reactions. The notion that any Negro could advance in the U.S. military drew doubts. Many of his critics wondered whether his advancement to E-4 was a response to the political pressure of the civil rights movement. They questioned whether he deserved this promotion. Not everyone in Carrollton was proud of what Byrd had achieved. He was glad to disappoint them.

The history of Byrd's work ethic in Carrollton spoke for itself. He and his family had built a reputation in Carrollton by working the cotton fields. They were known as hard workers and early risers. Byrd merely transferred that same energy to the decks of naval ships.

Getting into the U.S. Navy because of an executive order signed by President Truman was significant, but Byrd had to prove that his color was not the only reason why he was worthy of enlisting. Byrd was determined not only to be a sailor in uniform but also a sailor in a decorated uniform.

Many people in Carrollton could not understand Byrd's drive to become a great sailor in a white man's navy. Americans had made it clear that Negroes were inferior and were not welcomed in its finer institutions, especially the armed forces. They loved Byrd's uniform, but they were thrown by his motives and by the fact that a Negro was proud to wear what the white man tried to keep from him. Injustices and hostilities toward Negroes made the whole idea of a Negro sailor seem odd.

Nevertheless, Byrd did not see it from the same viewpoint. The glass was half full, not half empty. He chose to look past the negative and see the positive. For decades, Negroes were not permitted to wear the distinguishing mark of a proud American. Even if Truman had not stepped in, Byrd was ready to fight for his right to enlist. Indeed, Byrd cruised in by way of an executive order, but the chevron he now wore was through grit, determination, and effort.

In many ways, Truman's executive order had been a blessing and a curse. It was a blessing because Negroes were able to enlist, whereas initially they had been denied. Not only were they able to enlist, but they also were able to work in Navy ratings that did not involve mess duties. It was also a curse because the executive order carried a stigma.

Some white people felt that Negroes cruised into the military because of a weak president who buckled under political pressure. Of course, many of the Negroes did not see President Truman in the same light.

Despite the racial divide, Byrd had tunnel vision. He saw things the same way a sniper would see a target in his scope. His returning to Carrollton in uniform was a clear demonstration of progress in the U.S. military, even if that progress seemed to be minimal and slow moving. Annie Lloyd was proud and so were his three older brothers and sister.

Byrd did not make much of an impression on many of the adult whites when he returned in uniform. They thought he was a token Negro. The government had allowed him to advance in rate so that they could say that they were in compliance with the law. The same could not be said of many of the students of Stone Street High School. The day following his arrival, Byrd visited his old high school while dressed in uniform.

Numerous students were eager to hear his sea stories. Seeing the zeal in their eyes tugged at his heart. As God's destiny for him would have it, Byrd now found himself in the same position his recruiter was in, back in 1947, encouraging others to consider the benefits of joining the U.S. Navy.

With permission from the school administrators, Byrd was able to share his military experiences with many of the students. An audience of about seven young Negro men gathered around him. It was obvious that he was consumed by his life in the Navy. Byrd's fierce enthusiasm and sense of pride made him a perfect liaison between the Navy and future recruits. Inspiring would-be sailors was a welcome task. Byrd enjoyed talking about the U.S. Navy. The young men hoped that they could render service to their country as well.

The sharply dressed uniform continued to attract attention, and soon questions about what he did in the Navy followed. One of the students asked, "What are the two crossed anchors all about?" Byrd said, "Let me start by explaining the U.S. Navy rating structure. Two similar-sounding terms are used to describe Navy enlisted status, rate, and rating. Rate equates to military pay grade, and rating is one's occupational specialty." The captivated audience watched as Byrd pointed to his rating badge. First, he explained the V on his sleeve, "This is a chevron. It represents a petty officer third class (PO3). It is a rate as well as a pay grade. Each rating has its own specialty badge, which is worn on the left sleeve by all qualified persons in that field. The cross-anchors denote the boatswain's mate badge. Used in combination, the chevron and the cross-anchors symbolized a boatswain's mate third class." [47]

Midway through his presentation, Byrd was questioned about pay. All the sea stories were exciting, but many of the students wondered whether the adventures were worth it. Although leaving home in search of a better life was top priority for many of them, at the end of the day, the deciding factor was money. Byrd earnestly wanted his audience to consider the Navy, so he explained the pay grades. A pay grade constituted a numbering system from junior to senior and was linear across all five branches of the U.S. military. Byrd made it clear. The lowest military enlisted pay grade was E-1, and the highest was E-7. Officer pay grades in the Navy included W-1 through W-4 for warrant officers and O-1 through O-10 for officers. Enlisted Naval personnel may be promoted from enlisted to warrant officer status and in some cases directly to officer status. [48]

Along with presenting the incentive of pay, Byrd was careful not to sound too preachy when he explained what it meant to wear an armed forces uniform. In that, he still needed to drive home a critical philosophy. He had hoped to instill the importance of good character into the hearts and minds of his listeners. The uniform indeed brought distinction, but that distinction came with a heavy responsibility.

If a man or woman was to don the Navy uniform, he or she was to live out the Navy's philosophy. Wearing a uniform in the armed forces meant one had to have an upstanding lifestyle. As expected, his audience was a little less interested in the character building than they were of the pay grades. For a young Negro in the 1950s, currency was a strong motivator. The notion of character building seemed more conducive to church attendance, and most of the boys Byrd aimed to persuade attended services only because they were forced to go. Their disinterest in moral buildup however did not stop Byrd from pressing the issue.

The jump to becoming a petty officer would be less difficult if they had a strong understanding of the naval system. Byrd underscored the idea of leadership and drove home the point that good leaders grew out of being good followers. Some heard him, and some dismissed him. Since boot camp, Byrd worked hard to make the forged chain links of honor, morality, and virtue, which were wrapped around the fouled anchor, a natural part of his personality. He understood how important it was for young recruits to have character. Byrd was not annoyed by the attitude of his Stone Street High School family, but he was deeply concerned. He knew the value of opportunity.

If any of the students at Stone Street High School thought that their disinterest or impassivity in Byrd's emphasis on character building would soften his convictions or keep him from standing on the truth, they were mistaken. Those who wore the uniform had to be men of honor, and there was no getting around that fact. Byrd had been in the Navy only for three years, but it was as if he had spent most of his life on a Navy vessel. In the midst of racial tension, Byrd had been a standout sailor on both *Tarawa* and *Arcadia*. No one could deny that fact. He outperformed most of his competitors. In less than four years, Byrd had been promoted from seaman apprentice to petty officer third class, and he did not show any signs of stopping.

With his time winding down, Byrd made a specific reference to his rating badge, and he did it with a sense of urgency. He wanted to leave his audience with an imprint on their mind that their memory could never escape. If any of them aspired to join the Navy, Byrd was willing to be their sea daddy, mentoring them throughout their naval career. He knew what was necessary to succeed, especially in the boatswain's mate rating.

Besides the pay, what grabbed his listeners' attention was the fact that boatswain's mates were supervisors, even at the lowest pay grade of the petty officer (E-4). They were interested in learning that boatswain's mates supervised personnel in various ship maintenance duties. The idea of being a leader intrigued them. Boatswain's mates were the spine of the crew on a ship.

Byrd wanted the students to know that if they chose to enter the Navy, the possibilities of advancement, particularly in the boatswain's mate rating, were attainable. The journey would be no walk in the park, especially for young Negro men. Truman's executive order had opened the door, but the spirit of racism was still thriving. No one understood that better than Byrd. If they would trust in God and work hard, the possibility to advance existed. Byrd's allotted week of vacation went by rapidly, and he enjoyed his time off. A few days after his return from leave, he was transferred to *USS Smalley* (DD 565), the Fletcher- class destroyer.

SHERMAN AND WEEZ START A FAMILY

Sherman and Weez had much to celebrate the week of their first wedding anniversary. Weez was nine months pregnant, and the baby was due any day. Every night after dinner, they would go for a casual stroll down by the Battery, a scenic seawall fortified in the 1750's. A cool breeze seemed to meet them there every evening. On June 20, 1951, after their evening walk, Weez went into labor and Sherlyn Denise Byrd was born before midnight. Weez had combined the first four letters of Sherman's name, "Sher" with the "L" in Louise and came up with the name Sherlyn. She weighed 6 pounds, 11 ounces and was the apple of her father's eye. The birth of his daughter brought on an elevated sense of responsibility to Sherman. Every move from now on must count. Providing for Weez and the baby was his top priority.

He was grateful that the Lord had blessed him and Weez with a healthy baby girl. He bowed his head and said a prayer asking the Lord to give him the strength and means to always provide for them. Words cannot describe the feeling that comes with a firstborn child. The sky looked different. Sherman's sense of smell and touch magnified. He was bursting with life from the inside out. He was a father. Oh, happy day!

Their second wedding anniversary came on the heels of some other wonderful news. While assigned to *Smalley*, Sherman was advanced to Boatswain's Mate 2nd Class. He was grateful to God for allowing him to properly care for his family.

Eighteen months passed since the birth of their daughter Sherlyn. She started walking at 13 months. Many of their friends said that she was getting out of the way of her future brother or sister. Well, they were right. Weez got up from the sofa in the living room and headed back into the kitchen. Sherman watched her as she waddled a bit from side to side. He wanted her to stay still. She refused. It was the day before Christmas Eve, December 23, 1952, and she was nine months pregnant with their second child. The aroma of the sweet potato pies in the oven filled the room. Christmas was her favorite holiday. Weez enjoyed cooking enough food for her family, friends, and a few extra sailors. Word on the ship had spread that if a sailor was longing for a home-cooked meal that reminded him of his mother's, he needed to befriend Byrd. Weez had invited four sailors to join them for dinner on Christmas because they had no family in the area. It did not take long to tire of eating the food on the ship. So there she was, baking pies and wrapping gifts to put under the tree. Sherman was glad that he was on leave. At least he could entertain their daughter Sherlyn, who they called Shirley. Her greatest ambition in life was to follow her mother everywhere she went. Weez was feeling a little bit of pain that seemed like contractions, but they were so far apart that she thought it best not to say anything about it to Sherman. He would insist she sit down, and her pies would burn. Well, the baby inside of her womb had other plans. No sooner had she placed the two sweet potato pies on the ledge of her kitchen window than her water broke. Weez reluctantly gave in to the moment. She would have to leave her freshly picked collard greens, stemmed and unwashed, and go to the Naval Hospital.

Sherman Byrd Jr. was born at 10:35 p.m. on December 23, 1952. Weez checked for five fingers and five toes, as Sherman beamed with joy. God had blessed them with a healthy bouncing baby boy! He was the happiest man alive. Life was good. His wife and son were okay.

Shirley was happy with the doll baby she received and her handheld rolling toy that made popping sounds as she moved it around. Sherman made a mental note not to buy any other toys with loud sounds. He chalked the mistake up to being a fairly new father. Weez's mother Irene came by to finish cooking Christmas dinner for Sherman and the sailors. Sherman had established a routine of walking outside to meet the sailors who were about to enter his home. Come rain or shine he would greet them outside so that he could sternly remind them that there would be no cursing permitted in front of his wife, in-laws and children. He explained to them that he had to deal with being cursed at on a daily basis aboard the ship. What he endured was brutal. He would not tolerate the thought of his family having to go through the same thing. He knew he would not be able to shelter them in every situation, but he certainly had control of what was allowed to be said in his home. The young sailors quickly obliged and respected Sherman even the more. Dinner was served. They had turkey, ham, collard greens, macaroni and cheese, fresh rolls and sweet potato pie. Of course, there was that pot of rice. Southern girls love rice.

1954 WAS A GOOD YEAR

Weez was happy. She and Sherman had a small, yet comfortable, two-bedroom apartment on Reed Street, Charleston, South Carolina. It was within walking distance to her mother's house on South Street. Their daughter Shirley was three years old.

Sherman Jr. was now 20 months old. It was a rich man's family, as her girlfriend Bernadette would jokingly say. Weez and Sherman were far from being rich in material things, but what they did have was special. They were madly in love, and they worked well together. She was a conscientious mother and homemaker. Her skills in cooking, sewing, and keeping a clean house were second nature to her.

Weez laughed out loud as she thought about how nervous her stepfather Thomas would get every time Sherman came home from a tour at sea. He would say to her mother, "Irene, Weez will be pregnant again in three weeks." Irene would holler back at him and tell him to stop saying that.

Yes, Weez's man was coming home. This time, however, she did not have to worry about getting pregnant. She was already pregnant, six months. The baby was due sometime in November.

Shirley and Sherman were taking a nap. She had them on a schedule. Weez realized early on that she needed some quiet time on a daily basis. She sat on the couch and quietly began to thank the Lord for His goodness toward her and Sherman. The year 1954 was proving to be a good year for them. On January 12, Sherman was authorized to wear the Navy Occupation Service Medal for service in Europe commencing December 10, 1953.

Weez's mother Irene often stopped by their apartment to see how she was doing. As they cleaned collard greens while sitting at the kitchen table, her mother turned to her and said, "How are things going?" "Pretty good so far Momma," answered Weez. "Well, I want to encourage you to take time to find out the things that Sherman likes, and then make an effort do those things", said Irene. Weez smiled and said, "Yes Ma'am." She was grateful for their close relationship. At first Weez thought that it would be easy to follow that advice. But it was not. Most of the things he liked, she did not. He liked the traditions, rules, and regulations of the military, she liked making the latest style of dress. He liked football and reading, she liked trying new recipes and music. They both loved to dance. Through the first three years of their marriage, they began to melt together like two irons in a furnace. She learned about the Navy uniform, and the boatswain's mate pipe, and he learned how to change diapers and cook breakfast. At night after the children were asleep, or in the morning before they were awake, she learned to make his reading time and her sewing time. Her mother was saying to love Sherman to the point at which Weez preferred his happiness above her own. She should want to bring out the best in Sherman and help him to reach his full potential. When two people want the best for each other, then they will enjoy being in one another's presence. It was fun to hear how his day went at work. Sherman was not a complainer. He would set his mind on achieving a goal, and he would work at it until he did. Being raised working in cotton fields had taught him that there was a time and a season for everything. If it was not his time or season, then he ought to be preparing the soil. Then when the time came, he always would be ready.

Sherman's quest to advance to BM1 would put that theory to the test. He was recommended for advancement in January but was not selected. Sherman was disappointed but not discouraged. The teachers at Stone Street High School would often get them to chant: "If at first, you don't succeed, try, try, again." No, her husband was definitely not a quitter. She admired that about him, because neither was she.

On March 1, 1954, Sherman was authorized to wear a bronze star for his Second Good Conduct Award for service ending December 26, 1953. Not only did this medal attest to three years of superior behavior amid a barrage of racial injustices, but also his proficiency in rate. The Navy promptly recorded this military achievement.

Shirley was talking quite well now. Weez and Sherman decided to start calling each other momma and daddy, so that Shirley would say the same thing. It worked. Shirley stayed close to her mom all the time, often sleeping in the bed with them at night. Sherman Jr. was adventurous. He often was found touching, smelling, and looking for ways to take something apart. Weez child-proofed the apartment as safely as she could by moving harmful cleaning liquids and sharp objects to higher levels, out of their reach. All of her other decorative trinkets, she left right where they were, and taught them not to touch them. Children need to learn boundaries at an early age. Certain things they could not touch and certain places they could not go, both at home as well as when they were visiting others.

Weez felt that the woman sets the tone of the house. She can make it a happy atmosphere or a sad one. The children will follow her lead. Weez did everything she could to make sure the atmosphere in her home was a happy one. Whether the cupboard was full or just about empty, the children never knew, because eating biscuits and gravy was as joyful as eating chicken and rice. Weez knew how to stretch a meal. It was not about what they did or didn't have; it was about being loved and knowing they were loved. Setting a joyful atmosphere enabled Sherman and Weez to ensure that the children smoothly managed transitions between the times when Sherman was at home and when he was away.

USS SMALLEY

Smalley was awarded the Battle Efficiency Plaque for battle readiness exercises conducted from July 1, 1953, to June 30, 1954. All of the crewmembers were authorized to wear the letter E on their uniforms. Considered by many to be one of the most prestigious awards to which a sailor could contribute, Byrd was proud of the teamwork executed to secure their ships selection. This was a big deal. The crew worked long and hard to achieve this goal. The ship fulfilled its mission goals and excelled in ship handling, tactics, and weapon employment. On August 27, 1954, Byrd received commendation from the captain which stated, "It is considered that this award was due to the efforts of Sherman Byrd. Therefore the Commanding Officer takes pleasure in commending him for his outstanding performance of duty during this period set forth." The next day, the Captain's Meritorious Mast was held. The Commanding Officer said, "Sherman Byrd, BM2, U.S. Navy, demonstrated outstanding leadership and smart seamanship by hoisting the accommodation ladder when he became aware that *Smalley* was adrift and the mooring buoy was riding down the starboard side. By so doing, he prevented damage to the accommodation ladder and possible injury to the personnel working on it. For his outstanding performance of duty, I take pleasure in commending him."

Boatswain's Mate Chief Harvey Moore was proud of the things Byrd had accomplished while assigned to *Smalley*. As they sat near the anchor at the bow of the ship Moore said, "Byrd, I am very proud of the contributions you have made to make *Smalley* one of the best ships in the fleet. But as you and I both know, you cannot forge out a comfort zone here. During your last evaluation you mentioned to me that you would like to become a Navy diver. A deep sea diver class is getting ready to start in October." "I would like to volunteer", exclaimed Byrd! "First you will have to pass the required Physical Screening Test (PST)", said Moore. "I will do everything I possibly can to get your paperwork on the Captain's desk for his approval. I cannot make you any promises, but you will have my highest recommendation. You possess the skills and the aptitude to succeed as a U.S. Navy deep sea diver!" Three weeks later on September 20, 1954, Byrd transferred to U.S. Naval Station Guantanamo Bay (GTMO), Cuba, for PST.

CHAPTER SIX

PHYSICAL SCREENING TEST

G TMO was located on 45 square miles of land and water at Guantanamo Bay, Cuba. It was the oldest Navy base located outside of the continental United States, situated about 500 nautical miles away from Miami, Florida. The United States had leased GTMO in February 1903 to employ the bay as a coaling and naval station. The United States finalized a treaty with the Cuban government in December 1903. [49]

Byrd arrived at GTMO in September 1954 for the PST to become a Navy deep sea diver. GTMO was only one of a few naval bases that had a master diver as an instructor as well as a diving medical officer. Both people had to sign off the PST for the student to advance to Deep Sea Diver Training. Any unsatisfactory (UNSAT) grade for any portion of the PST disqualified the student. Byrd was determined to pass. The Navy did not have a lot of data on the effects of deep sea diving on Negroes. If Byrd were to successfully pass the prescreen test, he would be one of the first Negro specimens for them to study. Oh, what a specimen; he was now 5 feet, 11 inches tall, 180 pounds, lean, agile, strong, and intelligent. He could put to rest the theory that Negroes do not have the mental competence to succeed as a U.S. Navy Diver.

Before progressing to the mandatory prescreen test, the diving medical officer had to verify a few things. Failure in any one of the things would result in automatic disqualification from attending the school. First, he had to test Byrd's vision to ensure he was not colorblind. Second, Byrd was placed in a hyperbaric chamber to see whether he showed signs of the bends, also known as decompression sickness. Bends occur when dissolved gasses, mainly nitrogen from the diver's air tank are absorbed into body tissue as the diver descends and are then released as bubbles when the diver returns to sea level. The bubbles can adversely affect various areas of the body, the lungs, heart, and brain. [50] The bends could kill a diver. Byrd successfully passed both tests.

Next, he had to pass the swim test. The Navy taught Byrd how to perfect his breaststroke and sidestroke so that he used minimal effort. He had been swimming since the age of six, but he had never learned the right stroke techniques. Byrd was considered to be a strong and fast swimmer, but could he be a smart swimmer? He swam so effortlessly. Byrd really could be an asset to the Deep Sea Diver Team.

Byrd paced himself. One of the common errors of students screening for dive qualifications was to push too hard in the early examinations. Then they were too tired to complete the remaining portions of the test.

The swimmer was instructed to call out his name and lap number after each completed lap. Byrd glided through the water like a shark in search of prey. He displayed strength, potency, and energy. He performed the 500-yard swim in 12 minutes, 49 seconds time. Well below the 14 minutes allotted.

Byrd satisfactorily (SAT) completed the swim test. He then stood and rested for 10 minutes. Immediately following the rest period, the students were tasked to perform 42 push-ups in two minutes. Afterward, they could rest for two minutes. Byrd established a routine of doing pushups during boot camp, which helped to develop his upper-body strength.

He had textbook form. The requirements were that students keep their arms straight, with their backs, buttocks, and legs in line while in the push-up position. In the down position, their chests could not make contact with the deck, and their arms had to be at a right angle. Students could rest only while in the up position.

By the time two minutes had elapsed, Byrd was already standing. All 42 pushups were correctly performed. Byrd took his two minutes to rest. Next, he completed 50 sit-ups in two minutes. Then he rested two more minutes. No time limit was placed on performing the six pull-ups. After which he was allotted a 10-minute rest period.

All six potential students participating in the PST were in excellent physical condition. As the students lined up to perform the 1.5-mile run, Byrd took a spot in the rear. He had received a SAT for each exercise, with only one performance left to go. If he passed, he would be on his way to dive school in Washington, D.C. If he failed, he would be back on a ship in a boatswain's mate billet, but it would not be *Smalley*. When Byrd volunteered to be a Navy diver, he knew it was a nonreturnable billet. He would have to fit in wherever a spot was open. It was a risk he was willing to take. He had prayed about it, and he knew God would be with him. The whistle blew.

When the run started, Byrd shot past several of the students. He understood how complicated his situation was. He was the only Negro runner. Whatever he chose to do, he knew the tension would mount regardless. If he shot past all the runners, flexing his ability to float with the wind, it would confirm in the minds of his antagonists what they had been thinking all along. The onlookers would classify him as a strong, brute, savage beast from the lower primates in the jungles of Africa.

Byrd was far from naïve. He understood this racist thinking. But hanging back to allow the other runners to create distance would confirm an alternative theory that didn't sit well with him. Winning could stir up negative remarks, but losing was not acceptable. Besides, Byrd hated losing. He was never one to hold back.

Byrd settled on his course of action. It was the last of the qualification rounds. He paced himself and cruised through the 1.5-mile run. Once he completed the laps, Byrd hollered out "time." The timer called out Byrd's time, 12 minutes, 3 seconds. Byrd passed his PST.

After passing the prescreen tests in GTMO, Byrd received orders to transfer off *Smalley* and report for duty at the Deep Sea Divers C School located at the U.S. Naval Receiving Station, Washington 25, D.C. He had already completed 39 months of sea duty and had served 60 days outside the continental limits of the United States. Dive training was scheduled to start October 4, 1954, so Byrd was posted at GTMO until he could begin his formal training.

For Byrd, being transferred to Deep Sea Divers School was the climax to a good year. Upon his arrival, he would need to push past the prejudices as he had done before. The ghastliness of mistreatment would more than likely intensify. Byrd was aware of that possibility.

Negroes had multiple variations of skin tones. Some white people in the military stooped to the level of accepting lighter complexioned Negroes over others which were darker. They reasoned that if integration were unavoidable, then they would deal only with the lighter complexioned ones. Evidently, their mothers intermingled with a white man somewhere along the way. This tactic was not new. It also was used during slavery days. Slave owners preferred the house Negro to be a lighter complexion. They worked the darker Negroes in the field. Byrd's skin tone was often described as black, pitch black. He was not ashamed of his complexion. He was the same complexion as his mother. He was very much contented with that. She was one of the most beautiful people in the world, both inside and out. His skin color had nothing to do with his aptitude for learning or passion for getting the job done. He had every right to be trained as a deep sea diver, despite the opposition. President Truman had established that legal right. With the signing of Executive Order 9981 on July 26, 1948, President

Harry S. Truman made it possible for Byrd to receive equal treatment and opportunity in the U.S. Navy.

Although the president of the United States signed this executive order, Jim Crow, and all of his constituents, still had leverage. That spirit refused to budge or to dissipate. The executive order did not mean much to those who were dead-set on preventing him from ever making good use of it. To them, it was just another piece of paper.

When Byrd first arrived on base, he could sense the overall culture was no different from the culture he lived in while serving on *Tarawa* and *Arcadia*. It was no surprise to him; in fact, he had expected it. Things had begun to change on *Smalley*, however, because of Chief Moore. Chief Moore believed that they were all seaman. He often said that everybody had a job to do, and you dang well better know how to perform it. Change often begins with the chief. Although racial bias was the ruling order, Chief Moore knew that the atmosphere was ripe for the taking. If he treated Byrd with respect and impartiality, his petty officers and seaman had no choice but to follow suit. Byrd felt the same way, deep in his spirit. Byrd was determined to shake up the status quo. Negroes very rarely received recognition or awards. Chief Moore strived to make that a thing of the past.

ARRIVAL AT DEEP SEA DIVERS SCHOOL

Gunner's Mate Chief Paul Walton took a deep breath, settled back in his chair, and made circles with his thumbs. His eyes targeted a spot on the overhead. He thought, not here, not on my watch.

Seemed no one in the elite unit, especially Walton, rooted for Negroes to join them.

They were a sacred brotherhood. Rubbing his index finger beneath his nose, he already could smell the sweat. Niggers smelled different. Oh, how disgusting.

The U.S. Naval Gun Factory in Washington, 25, D.C., was a 125-acre, 200-building plot that embosomed the heart of the Anacostia River. Walton heard that BM2 Sherman Byrd had arrived at Naval Receiving Station (NAVRECSTA). He was enrolled in his Deep Sea Divers C School. This was a catastrophe. An outrage, or at least that's what his brain kept howling. Who allowed a Negro to enter dive school––the most privileged and dominant diving school in the United States?

Walton frowned. He sighed. Nothing was funny about this "new" America. The Negroes somehow had infiltrated the political fabric of his great country. He gazed up, shaking his head. He felt a strong shiver of contempt permeate throughout his body. Anxiety stood parallel to his disgust. That darn executive order.

What else, as if that wasn't enough? Those Negroes wanted equal voting rights. They wanted the "Whites Only" signs at water fountains and restrooms to come down. Politics had now slithered into the military. His beloved Navy, the branch of service he had served with pride and passion, had placed him in a crucible, one that would either make or break his career.

Walton, grit his teeth. He was about to make history, although he had no desire to, at least not in this manner. He was about to become one of the first CPOs in the U.S. Navy to allow a Negro, one not capable of understanding compressors, decompression tables, and diving physics, to attend the elite Naval Deep Sea Divers School. Not this chief!

On the yard, resistance was swift and animated. The air of hostility at the Naval Gun Factory was high. That Negro wouldn't stand a chance.

At 9:00 a.m., on September 30, 1954, Byrd marched into the personnel unit at the U.S. Naval Gun Factory, chin up and shoulders level. A few of the white sailors were appalled at his bold entry. His white Crackerjacks were sharply pressed, and the knot on his neckerchief was a perfect cube. The standard Navy-issue sea bag hung tightly over his left shoulder, and his service record was firmly clutched in his right hand. Byrd was ready for duty.

He dropped his bag to the deck and stepped forward to request assistance from the on- duty yeoman. As he had expected, a faint chatter, which was more like a deep and menacing murmur, had already filled the hall. Byrd had seen and experienced much worse when he was first stationed on *Tarawa*. He quietly asked God, "When will this hatred end?" He shook himself. This was not the time or the place to question the road that God so lovingly and purposefully led him down. God was faithful in keeping him safe thus far, and Byrd was confident that his grace would continue to be with him.

Walton realized that it would be impossible to keep Byrd segregated from the other 24 white deep sea diver candidates. The school was centered on camaraderie, brotherhood and professionalism. Throughout the 1940s, the Navy's campaign was to bar the Negroes from all significant ratings. Walton felt the 1950s should follow the same pattern. Apparently, the Truman administration did not agree.

It was apparent that Walton had ignored the obvious. Negroes were on the rise; they demanded integration, and they would not be stopped. That included Byrd. A few months earlier in May 1954, the Supreme Court under the direction of Chief Justice Earl Warren unanimously ruled that segregation in the public school system was unconstitutional. That Negro Attorney Thurgood Marshall had proved that separate Negro public schools were not equal to their white counterparts in the case of Brown v. the Board of Education.[51]

Walton reasoned that the longstanding policy of World War II on military segregation should be upheld. But he failed to recognize that the foundation and structure of racial divides in civilian life had collapsed. Byrd was a vivid reminder that change had come.

Byrd was an avid sailor with a bounce in his step and way too much confidence. Walton felt a surge of disgust and outrage at what he believed to be bravado. From that point forward, he made it his personal mission to obstruct Byrd's progress. The E-5 may have had a dream, but the E-7 was going to turn it into a nightmare. Walton hated his confidence and took it as a personal attack against the elitism that had defined the Deep Sea Divers C School.

Byrd had arrived on base with the drive to become a deep sea diver. His service record spoke volumes about his character and initiative, so it was more than possible, even probable, that Byrd could pull off the unthinkable. This possibility was incompatible with Walton's worldview. In his mind, he believed Negroes were good only for lifting bales of hay, plowing fields, and other hard labor.

Byrd's presence angered Walton. He knew Byrd was a worthy candidate, but he couldn't escape the reality that a Negro, smart as he may have been, was now a part of his dive school. If he graduated, he'd be a part of a fellowship of deep sea divers, a sacred brotherhood.

Walton continued to observe Byrd work hard to adapt to the early challenges of training, as well as to the thick racial tension that had ballooned ever since he arrived. As far as he was concerned, Byrd was welcomed at the dive school as much as a Japanese pilot. The Negro from Mississippi was his personal Pearl Harbor. And because Chief Walton didn't want him at the school, he worked him as if Byrd was a slave on a plantation.

Walton wasted no time putting Byrd in his place, a position he thought was made for a Negro. If he were not going to be a mess cook, then he would need to be a hard labor guy in some other capacity. And besides, he was the new kid on the block. Byrd knew the work he was assigned was much more than just rookie hazing. He immediately was handed a swab and a bucket, and a detailed description of how Chief Walton wanted the head cleaned with a clear message that he would have no help. He was on his own.

Byrd complied and voiced no complaint. He had learned to take his lumps early in life. Being given the dirtiest jobs had become a regular routine during his Navy career. Even with President Truman's executive order signed and approved, Byrd knew that the reality of integration in his life would sprout slowly. This growth would take some time. He was a man just like they were.

Byrd was aware that he was an unwanted intruder, a marked man. It wasn't as if the mood was a secret. But, his radical and determined nature would not allow Chief Walton or any of the others to crush his will. It would never happen. He was on a divine assignment. God had called him to be a chief, a silent professional.[52]

As he swabbed the deck, Byrd couldn't help but think about how a "hard work" mentality consumed him. It was in his blood. The head would glisten even if he had to work until midnight. Byrd remembered when his family did not have an indoor bathroom in their house. So, cleaning the head did not have as much of an adverse effect on him as they thought it would. Byrd chose to focus on the positive things in a situation, he was grateful that God had given him an opportunity to become a U.S. Navy deep sea diver. If he could move beyond the ignorant racist crap they were going to throw his way, he could concentrate on passing the physical and intellectual tests required to be a deep sea diver. Hopefully, the next Negro sailor to attend the school would be accepted for the man that he was and not be discriminated against because of the color of his skin.

CHAPTER SEVEN

BUY-IN (DEEP SEA DIVERS SCHOOL)

The shifting tide of American race relations had put Chief Walton into a strange and vulnerable position. It seemed everyone from an outhouse to the White House had taken a firm grasp of the issue and had pushed the agenda further than Walton would have liked to see it go.

The campaign to make Byrd feel as if he were a vital part of the unit was excruciating. Training Byrd was one thing, but adopting him as a brother was something altogether different. It only heightened Walton's displeasure. Handling the possibility of calling a Negro, a brother was traumatizing to Walton. He was not accustomed to associating with Negroes, and he certainly did not wish to start now.

Every time Walton thought of orchestrating an unwarranted Byrd departure, he gazed at himself in uniform. He was a chief in the U.S. Navy, the world's finest. Part of his responsibilities as a chief was to persuade the lower enlisted men to buy into the campaign. Deep sea divers were a brotherhood. Theoretically, that would include Byrd, a thought that he wished he could deep six, just like preparing a grave in a cemetery.

The weight around his neck was heavy. He tilted his head and took a deep sigh. Walton was looking for something that could justify his prejudice. At the same time, he was trying to ensure the buy-in of his protégés without losing his "whiteness" or forfeiting the respect of his petty officers.

The reactions coming from the Goat Locker, a restricted getaway place for chiefs only, sure did not help any. It was appalling. His brothers in the Goat Locker already had made it clear, whether through contempt or comedy, how they felt about his assignment. It would spell disaster if the other dive students followed suit. He could always push an agenda, but that was not exactly what he wanted. As the dive instructor, he had to ensure that all divers worked as a team, and that would include Byrd.

Walton was trying hard to look beyond the pending challenge, knowing that he could not avoid it. He stood and paced the Goat Locker. He understood that although achieving buy-in was a mandatory task; it was also possibly the epilogue to his outstanding naval career. If not, it was a death sentence on his influence amid his colleagues. Getting the other white dive candidates to buy-in to training with Byrd was critical to prolonging reasonable race relations in the Navy. Walton knew the Navy could no longer afford token integration. He could not look to the Army or the Marines for moral support either. In both branches, Negroes had gained traction, and by the end of the war, they were primed to hold positions previously given exclusively to whites.

Walton felt lost, even though the executive compass had made the point of direction clear. Obey the administrative order or suffer the severest of sanctions. He hated his predicament. Leaving the Navy was not an option. Therefore he had no choice but to bite the bullet and motivate his subordinates to accept a Negro into their brotherhood.

Part of the dilemma Walton faced was convincing his subordinates, as well as his colleagues, to bury racist stereotypes. That stereotype was that Negroes, especially those from the South, did not have the faculties needed to succeed in the elite schools. Byrd was different, however. His service record provided proof that he did not fit into those stereotypes. Motivating the other students to accept integration was a herculean task.

Gunners Mate Second Class Tony Williams and Machinist Mate Second Class Andrew Smith approached Walton while he was walking toward his car to leave the school. They were two of the deep sea diver students in the same class as Byrd. "Chief Walton, can we talk to you for a minute," Williams asked? "Sure," answered Chief Walton. " Well, Smith and I could not hold the anger and disgust we are feeling inside any longer! We had to come and get it off of our chests. Under no circumstances should a white man be kneeling down and putting on a nigger's shoes! We are not his servants", said Williams. "Stop, hold it right there!" shouted Chief Walton as he held his right hand up like a traffic cop. "That is exactly what you are! Both of you! So is Byrd! We are all, servants one to another. Not only will we lace up his shoes, as if he were a prince, but we will place the Mark V diving helmet on his head as if he were a king. We will make sure his equipment is clean and working properly, enjoying every moment of our labor. We will love him like a brother, and if you two do not want to do that then you cannot be a deep sea diver! So you all go home now and think about it. If you change your mind about putting on those shoes, I will see you in class tomorrow", shouted Walton. The two men abruptly turned around and stomped off in the opposite direction. Walton could not pacify the young sailor's emotions. They had a mission to accomplish. The words he spoke did the work of a two edged sword, it swung forward to pierce deep into their prejudices, and then jolted backward to cut into his hypocrisy.

Williams and Smith showed up for class the next day, but they were still not happy about the situation. It was hard not to demonstrate the anger on their faces. As they prepared to assemble the Mark V dive suit on Byrd, Walton overheard Williams say to Byrd, "Your Momma is dumb, she can't read or write, and your sister is a house nigger, only good for being the

Master's midnight mistress." Byrd's jawbone tightened but he did not say a word, as Williams and Smith chuckled amongst themselves. Men who were hotheaded and unable to control their temper were dismissed from the school. Lack of patience and a flaring temper would put the other divers at risk. Staying alive and completing the mission were the top two priorities of every job assignment. Walton remained silent. He wanted to see how Byrd would handle the situation. He certainly could not protect him from the slew of racial remarks that were yet to come. Byrd felt anger building up inside of him. Williams could belittle him all day and night, but disrespecting his mother and sister was a punch in the gut. Byrd assessed the situation. Clearly Williams was trying to provoke him to lose his temper and be disqualified from deep sea dive school. Byrd knew that there were times in life when you have to pick your fights. This was certainly one of those times. Byrd chose not to fight this one. He would better honor his mother and sister by passing the class than punching Williams in the mouth. He remained calm by quietly repeating one of his favorite bible verses in his mind, "Thou wilt keep him in perfect peace, whose mind is stayed on thee: because he trusteth in thee." [53] Byrd took a deep breath and trusted God.

Divers rotated the task of assembling the Mark V dive suit onto each other. Correct assembly was a matter of life and death and had to be done right the first time, all of the time. Walton knew the other divers were repulsed at the sight of Byrd's dark skin. He understood because he shared the same sentiment. Regardless of how they felt, the line was already drawn in the sand. The diving students must jell together as one.

Military protocol demanded that the chief, an E-7, maintain a supervisory influence over the E-1s to E-6s and he had to be cautious not to fraternize with Williams and Smith because it would affect his ability to do his job. Walton needed to maintain a supervisor-subordinate relationship with the students, while simultaneously making sure they knew he would lay down his life for them. After all, divers were brothers. His ability to make that distinction among the students would be the difference between the divers buying into the necessity of teamwork and refusing to perform their sworn duties. Walton did another sweep through Byrd's service record, looking for any loophole that would disqualify him. He found nothing. As the clock ticked away, his anxiety heightened.

Executive Order 9981 was now seven years old. The equal treatment of all races in the armed forces was not being accomplished at the rate expected. Resistance to the order was deeply rooted in the hearts of those who were against integration. Walton's Deep Sea Divers School class consisted of 24 white students and one Negro student. Walton grappled with his inability to get the 25 students to mesh. No matter how many excuses he came up with during his analysis of the situation, it all boiled down to this: he had not yet meshed with the Negro student. His students would never demonstrate brotherhood until he showed them the way. Things must start and finish with the chief.

Nothing can bring a group of hardnosed, strong-willed sailors together the way performing artificial respiration on each other can. First aid was scheduled for the fourth week of class, but Walton decided to move it up to the second week. He did not have a moment to spare. If he did not get these men to accept one another, regardless of the color of their skin, then the class will be a failure. Walton would have failed his superiors, students, and himself. Whenever orders came down from his senior officer, it was his responsibility to get the students to accept them. No matter how unpleasant or difficult the task, he must be enthusiastic to comply and require his men to follow suit. He squirmed at the thought of his hands touching Byrd's body. Oh God, what had the world become! One thing was for sure, if he expected to deliver to the Navy the highly trained divers that they so desperately needed, he had better get a grip on it.

For a solid week, day after day, Walton had his students training in the classroom for the first four hours of the day and then practicing what they had learned when they returned from lunch. "Alright, listen up", said

Walton in a loud voice. "I need all of you to lay flat on your backs in a straight line, separated by an arms-length. Today we are going to perform artificial respiration on one another. I will be evaluating your proficiency. You are to assume that your classmate has drowned. He is not breathing and in need of help to prevent possible brain damage or loss of life." Some of their faces told the story. Although their voices said, "yes, chief," their body language said something different. The frowns and the wide eyes of disbelief varied, but all meant the same thing. They did not want to do it. They would have to touch Byrd's hands, face, back and arms. Two of them gagged at the thought. Walton shouted, "If I so much as see one drop of vomit come out of either of your mouths, you will be dismissed from the class!" He looked directly at Williams and said "Try me! You better swallow every drop of it!" Williams pinched his nose and began to swallow the vomit in his mouth. Byrd cringed as his knees buckled. He thought to himself, this is it, I can't take it anymore, I am going to walk out of the door and never look back! How can a man hate me so much that the thought of touching my body would make him vomit? He does not know me! The way I am feeling right now, I could break his neck with my bare hands! Help me God! I don't think I'm going to make it! At that very moment, the deep sea dive student who stood on Byrd's right hand side, reached up and put his left hand on Byrd's right shoulder, gripping it firmly. Byrd did not know his name. He looked Byrd directly in his eyes. Without verbalizing one word, his eyes said it all, "Hold on my brother, don't walk away, I am with you!" The dive student on Byrd's left-hand side reached out his right hand and placed it on Byrd's left shoulder, also gripping it firmly. Byrd felt as if some of the strength within his two classmates transferred into him. He straightened up both of his knees. He would not buckle, he would not fall. God gave him the strength not to walk away. When he looked around the room, he saw how a chain of linked hands on shoulders had formed on each side. Not everyone, but they were the majority. Byrd was not alone!

Walton's voice cracked the thick tension in the room. He said, "I will take the lead and demonstrate the proper way to perform artificial respiration." He ordered them to assume their positions. They laid flat on the ground, and one by one, he performed artificial respiration on each student. Byrd was seventh in line. Walton went through the steps without flinching. He had to. His students needed to see how important the mission was to him. He was able to set aside the prejudices instilled in him since childhood, and he wanted them to do the same. He would never ask any one of his students to do something he wouldn't do himself. By the time Walton reached the end of the line, he motioned for the students to start. For five straight days, they performed this drill.

The students experienced a breakthrough. He wasn't sure which day it occurred. He did not care. The group began to jell, different people for different reasons. The drill forced each of them to make a choice, even Byrd. This was no cakewalk for him either. Although some of the students had to overcome their reluctance to touch Byrd, he had to push past what he was feeling 24 times. If a student could not overcome this situation, he certainly would not be able to deal with the inevitable horrors he would see recovering bodies from air plane crashes and shipwrecks. Chief Walton was prepared to release any one of them from the program, if they could not complete this task. The rubber had met the road. By the time the First Aid Class ended, all divers had resolved to show compassion rather than disgust, to give life rather than take it.

CONDUCT AND CAPTAIN'S MAST

Navy chiefs have effectively turned numerous sailors young and old from wayward conduct. The harsh discipline of a chief has saved many naval careers. Byrd's climb up the ladder would be no different.

Byrd had been an exemplary sailor, one who illustrated the characteristics and values of the U.S. Navy. He was an intense individual. His ability to manifest the Navy's principles and standards did not come as a surprise to anyone who knew him personally. Being a sharp sailor came naturally to him.

Byrd's history of good conduct did not start at the Naval Recruiting Station in Greenwood, Mississippi, nor did it start when his bus rolled into the U.S. Naval Recruit Station in Little Rock, Arkansas. He had learned good conduct and hard work in Carrollton, Mississippi, under the watchful eyes of his mother. He had spent many evenings carefully watching her character and resolve. This gave him an example on which he would base his own standards.

He took note of how his mother had responded to the owner of the cotton fields where she and her boys worked Monday through Friday from sunup to sundown. Despite the ordeal of severe back pain she never complained. She showed great appreciation to the owner. "Don't bite the hand that feeds you," she would say. "Life is better for me than it was for my mom and dad. If you trust God, it will be better for you than it was for me." Her character had tremendous influence over him.

Byrd decided that if given the chance to get out of the cotton fields of Carrollton, he would take it. In 1947, the U.S. Navy granted him that opportunity. He would follow his mother's example, and not bite the hand that would feed him.

Since the first week of dive training, Byrd held firm to his conviction of conducting himself properly. Whether motivated by a deep sense of honor for his parents or some loftier purpose, Byrd focused hard on maintaining his demeanor. Even while suffering under tremendous racial tension, Byrd knew that his attitude would only benefit him.

For the help he needed, he turned his thoughts toward God. Not only did his mother teach him how to conduct himself amid adversity, she also taught him how to pray and stay connected to the bishop of his soul.

Day by day he reminded himself that he was right where God wanted him to be. He was not alone. The same God that kept him safe in the cotton fields of Mississippi, home of the Ku Klux Klan, would keep him safe at the Navy's Deep Sea Divers School. His relationship with God kept him grounded.

Byrd's conduct had been tested rigorously within the first couple of weeks of dive training. Nevertheless he had learned to master his emotions. Through most of his close encounters he came out unscathed. His actions remained above reproach. On March 2, 1955, however, Byrd underwent a test that marred his otherwise squeaky clean record.

The test took place outside a tavern near 7th and S Street NW, Washington, D.C., not too far from the famed Crystal Caverns and Howard University campus. It was about a half-hour past midnight. The incident involved Byrd and two Negro men from the local area. A couple of the young ladies at the tavern had tried unsuccessfully to get Byrd's attention. He was content to just wind down, drink a couple of beers, and listen to a little jazz. The rigors of Deep Sea Divers School had filled him with steam and the valve had to be relieved. One of the locals, who had been jilted in his own advances toward one of the young ladies, was irritated by her flir-tatiousness toward Byrd. The local went over to where she was sitting and grabbed her by the arm! "Come on, dance with me!" he said. The young lady shouted in an aggravated voice, "Ralph you need to keep your hands off of me! I do not want to dance!" Ralph's behavior toward the young lady became progressively more abusive. So much so, that Byrd felt obligated to intervene.

"Hey man, you are hurting her! Let her go!" said Byrd. "You better mind your own business before I put my hands on you!" hollered Ralph. The tavern owner quickly intervened. He told Ralph to go and sit down and leave the young lady alone. The mood in the tavern changed and Byrd knew that it was time for him to go. The last thing he needed was to be kicked out of diving school because of some immature locals. As he exited the tavern, the two locals followed him outside. The faster he walked, the faster they walked. Byrd could not believe what was about to go down. Here he was a month away from graduating from Deep Sea Divers School with a spotless record and it could all go down the drain in a matter of minutes. All for what, a young lady whose name he did not know?

The two locals quickly caught up to him. Ralph threw the first punch. His friend threw the second. Byrd had no time to talk his way out of the predicament. He had to resort to what he knew. Without saying a word he threw a flurry of punches. Ralph hit the sidewalk. His friend wiped the blood flowing from his lip. Sirens from a police car whined in the background. The friend took off running. Byrd peered down at the sidewalk. Ralph was not moving. The police pulled up as Byrd was reaching down to check for a pulse. They ordered him to stand back as they assisted Ralph. One of the officers took Byrd's statement about what had just happened. To Byrd's surprise, after he came to, Ralph actually told the truth about how things went down. The police officers made the decision to turn Byrd over to his chief instead of arresting him. Byrd did not know which of the consequences was worse, going to jail or facing the wrath of the chief.

Just thirty minutes earlier Byrd had finally taken a moment to relax from the tremendous strain racism had him under. The moment he let down his guard, he became involved in a street fight. It all happened so fast. All of the studying and training had just gone down the drain.

Even though Byrd was not arrested, Walton could dismiss him from the program. The officers cited him for unruly conduct. Local police often turned skirmishes involving sailors over to their chief. The chief's disciplinary measures were far more critical to instilling the lessons the sailors needed to learn. Byrd assessed the situation. He had a 90 percent chance of being kicked out of Deep Sea Divers School. As he sat in the back of the police squad car, Byrd hung his head.

Walton met the police officers at the entrance gate of the Navy Yard. He did not look too happy to be up and in uniform at 1:30 in the morning.

After talking with the police officers for a few minutes, Byrd was turned over into his custody. As they walked back toward the barracks, Byrd was granted permission to tell his side of the story. Walton listened but gave no signal as to what his response to the altercation would be.

The police report sparked an investigation in accordance with the pretrial procedure of the Uniform Code of Military Justice (UCMJ). Byrd's chain of command did not make any quick judgments. It was standard operating procedure to abide by the due process guidelines of the UCMJ before bringing formal or informal charges.

Although it was not necessary as a part of its investigation, the command held a disciplinary review board to determine whether Byrd was to be ordered to Captain's Mast (Article 15). Once the inquiry was complete, the command determined that he violated Article 114 of the UCMJ for his participation in a fight. At that point, Byrd faced nonjudicial punishment (NJP). [54]

On March 15, 1955, the Commanding Officer of the U.S. Naval Receiving Station, Washington 25, D.C. summoned BM2 Sherman Byrd and held Captain's Mast for the disorderly conduct committed on March 2 at or around 7th and S Street, NW, Washington, D.C. Byrd did not refuse NJP and accepted the action offered by his command. Acting Discipline Officer Lieutenant E. W. Etheridge administered the action.

Although Byrd felt justified in his actions, he did not want to reject Article 15 in favor of a court martial. It was too risky. Even with the best legal counsel, there was always a chance he could be released with a dishonorable discharge. Off the record, Negroes still were not welcome in the military. So, he was more than willing to take the punishment from his command.

The main reason Byrd chose to accept mast was that he knew his command was limited in the degree of punishment it could allot. Byrd had familiarized himself with the UCMJ and its articles and procedures. He wanted the Navy to see him as one who was committed to the highest level of military authority. That meant he had to abide strictly by the military's codes. Byrd was ready to stand before his commanding officer and explain his account of the events.

Byrd knew his Booker Rights (NJP rights), so he elected to decline legal counsel before he accepted NJP, even when he was informed he was able to confer with the judge advocate general. He had every right to refuse mast according to the Booker Rights, but he opted to take responsibility and to own up to what the UCMJ considered misconduct. Accepting responsibility was another lesson he had learned from his mother. Now more than ever, Byrd knew he would need to show the Navy that he was a responsible sailor, one worthy of being a part of the family of deep sea divers.

Although he declined legal counsel, the Legal Officer still would be present at the proceedings when Byrd would stand and face the charges levied against him. It was standard procedure. Lieutenant Etheridge thoroughly reviewed Byrd's service record, and he was equally impressed with his accomplishments as was Walton.

Byrd was in his dress uniform when he mustered at Captain's Mast at the Main Navy Yard Building on Constitution Avenue. It was at 9:00 a.m. Once at the building, he immediately felt an eerie sort of tension. This was a low point in his naval career, at least officially. Despite the anxiety he felt, he knew that taking responsibility for his actions would have a favorable outcome. His mother had established this foundation, teaching him that the God of Abraham, Isaac, and Jacob would show mercy, if he told the truth.

After all, He was the God of Truth and He could not bless a lie.

Walton accompanied Byrd to the proceedings, as required by a chief. Whether the accusations were true or false, as his chief, he always would stand by his side. He hoped Byrd knew that he was not alone. Byrd's conduct, on and off base was a reflection of Walton's leadership. He needed to evaluate what he could have done differently to prevent Byrd from receiving this negative mark on his service record. Did Byrd obey or disobey instructions? Not everything was clear-cut black and white. Some situations fall in gray areas. This was one of those times. As his chief, it was his responsibility to assess the difference.

It did not matter to Walton that this was the perfect opportunity to get rid of Byrd once and for all. He would have been well within his rights to kick Byrd out of the Deep Sea Divers School. God has a strange way of opening the eyes of those who are blind. The whole situation forced Walton to see the error of his ways. Byrd was defending himself. He did not run away. He stayed to ensure that his attacker was okay. Byrd made him aware of the predicament in a timely manner and made no excuses for what happened. Walton considered that perhaps bad things could happen to good people.

Walton knew how important graduating from Deep Sea Divers School was to Byrd. He had passed every physical and written test given to him thus far. Whatever Walton asked him to do, he did it. If he saw something that needed to be done, he would do that too. He was an initiator. He was a go-getter. So there Walton stood, posted on the left-hand side of Lieutenant Etheridge, the discipline officer, and the right-hand side of Byrd. Chiefs are silent professionals, standing in the gap between officers and petty officers. Being a chief is not for the weak-minded. They bear the heavy load of their unit's trials and tribulations on a daily basis.

Walton hoped that Lieutenant Etheridge would turn Byrd over to him for action as he had recommended. Chiefs do not discipline, but rather they train their petty officers and seaman by administering extra instruction to bring them back to the "Navy way" of doing things. [55] Most chiefs are wise beyond their years. He already had a list of administrative instructions prepared for Byrd. Walton was more than capable of brow-beating his petty officers, but he certainly did not want anyone else to do it.

The lieutenant stood at the podium as he read off Article 31b of the UCMJ, which was the equivalent of the Miranda rights law enforcement officers read to suspects under arrest. [56] Lieutenant Etheridge's threatening voice filled the room. Byrd remained calm. He was prepared to hear the evidence and was primed to offer a strong defense.

Byrd had exercised his right to defend himself when attacked. Yet, he and Walton were well aware that the command could not simply look the other way. The absence of punishment would send the deep sea diver class the wrong message. By military standards, the infraction was minor but Byrd still had violated the UCMJ.

More than anything, Byrd did not want to be suspended from duty. A suspension would serve him a crushing blow at a critical time. He was less than one month away from advancing out of dive school, and a suspension would set him back at least a year or two. Ultimately, this blotch on his record could keep him from reaching his goal of one day becoming a chief in the U.S. Navy. It was common knowledge that a Negro had to perform above the standards of a white man just to be considered equal. The thought of ruining the chances for other Negroes who possibly could follow in his footsteps haunted him. Most devastating for Byrd was that he knew the command had the right to hand down a suspension. If God did not help him out of this shattering situation, he did not stand a chance.

When Lieutenant Etheridge read off the evidence found in the inquiry, Byrd did not contest. As the hearing unfolded, he began to get the sense that the command did not want to hammer him. If it were not for the official need of Captain's Mast, he believed the command might have given him a pass. According to the chain of command, his actions did not shed a good light on the Deep Sea Divers School program. That alone warranted his receiving a blotch on his service record, small as it may have been.

Byrd could tell that the wheels were turning inside the mind of Lieutenant Etheridge. Before he made a decision, he gave Byrd an opportunity to explain his side of the story. The command heard what had happened and had launched a thorough investigation, but they needed to hear from Byrd officially. This was likely Byrd's opportunity to give the command a glimpse of his mind-set and personality, something neither Lieutenant Etheridge nor the other officers could glean from his service record.

With much accuracy, Byrd explained the incident. His commentary was sound and methodical. At some point in the commentary, Byrd could see God's favor settling in the room. It showed on the faces of his interrogators, especially Lieutenant Etheridge. The expression on the legal officer's face told the whole story. Byrd had the capacity to defend himself, and not just with his hands when under attack, apparently, but also with his mind when facing the courts.

After Byrd's defense, Lieutenant Etheridge dismissed Captain's Mast and the NJP allotted four days' restriction without suspension of duty. Walton's presence in the room had a lot to do with Byrd not receiving a suspension. He did not let his personal prejudices interfere with his responsibilities. As a chief, he was required to correctly assess all types of situations. If Byrd had deserved a harsh punishment for his actions, Walton would have been the first one to tell him. On the other hand, if Byrd deserved leniency, he would speak to the other officers on Byrd's behalf. [57]

Even with Captain's Mast settled, passing Deep Sea Divers School was still not a done deal. Byrd had less than 30 days to go. The rest of his time at the school would have to progress without disruptions. The ball was in his court. Byrd thanked Walton for standing with him during Captain's Mast. Walton told him, "You may want to hold on to that thank you until after you complete the extra administrative instructions I'm about to issue." There was no smile on his face.

CHAPTER EIGHT

A MOMENT OF CHOICE

There they were, one standing, one sitting. One white, one Negro, eyes locked, daring the other to blink. One of them would ruin their naval career today. He unjustifiably would be branded a failure all because of a single moment of choice. One would continue to receive training, but no advancement. He undoubtedly would be given additional responsibilities, but no recognition —simply because of a single decision that had to be made.

Despite the 70-degree weather and the 7 knots of wind speed, the water of the Anacostia River seemed to react to the tenseness in the air. Waves crashed against the side of the diving rig. Walton, a master diver, and Byrd, a deep sea diver student, were facing a crucial moment in their lives that challenged all they knew about where they had come from and where they were headed.

It was Friday, April 1, 1955, and Walton was on the verge of becoming one of the first chiefs to allow a Negro to graduate from Deep Sea Divers School. The extra miles of running and swimming Walton assigned to Byrd made him stronger. Forty percent of his "other duties as assigned" involved cleaning the head, which he executed with the same meticulous detail as cleaning the equipment after a dive.

Walton was caught between a rock and a hard place. Should he honor the tradition of his father who hated Negroes and believed they could not be trusted? "Coons," he called them. The whiteness of their eyeballs against the blackness of their skin reminded him of the rings around the eyes of the raccoons; the same animals he hunted and skinned in the woods of Alabama. Or should he embrace the "tradition of the chief," as one who makes a fair and accurate assessment of the knowledge and abilities of each man under his instruction? After all, the gold color on the sleeves of the Navy uniform he so proudly wore represented integrity. Could his commitment to professionalism extend far enough to acknowledge that Byrd had not only met but excelled at all of the requirements necessary to qualify him as a First Class Deep Sea Diver?

Integrity, slapped Walton in the face. If he allowed Byrd to pass the class, it would mean killing his own career. He had reached the pinnacle of the enlisted rates. He was an E-7, and there was nothing higher. He dreamed of one day crossing over into the officer rank. This one decision could eliminate his opportunity to advance into the Chief Warrant Officer or Limited Duty Officer programs. Walton felt sick to his stomach. He already was the butt of jokes in the Chief's Mess. They called him "nigger lover," "coon kisser," and many other horrible things. He felt helpless. There was nothing he could do. He had a family, a wife, two daughters, and a son. This decision ultimately would affect their way of life, too. It was a lose-lose situation.

For 25 weeks, the students endured brutal training. The original class of 25 students was now down to 17. Each one of the young men had clung to his every word. They were gunner's mates, boatswain's mates, machinist's mates, and metal smiths. All had the hopes of joining a fraternity of brothers who accepted the possibility that on any given day at work, they could die. These men were willing to descend to the depths of the ocean and encounter unknown dangers to complete any mission. It was an honor to be counted among them. They knew their brother would be swift to die to keep the other safe. It was one thing to pass a test in class and execute a practice drill to perfection. It was another thing to make your wife a widow and your children fatherless in a moment.

No matter how much he wanted to get out of this responsibility, he was the chief and the master diver. The decision was his to make. How would he be able to look the other diver candidates in the eye if Byrd failed the class? They knew he was the fastest; they knew he was the strongest. He had remained even-tempered throughout his training, despite the barrage of insults about his sister and mother. Byrd was determined to finish what he had started. Byrd was not the best Deep Sea Diver in Class 02B-55, but he definitely was in the top10. He was on target to finish seventh. This final dive was going to be like a practice drill for him. Disassembling and reassembling a pipe with flanges while submerged under 60 feet of water was something he had done successfully time and time again. "Confidence" should have been Byrd's first name. It exuberated in his walk and job performance. He was among a class of some of the finest young men the Navy had to offer.

Walton had to admit to himself that he had been wrong. Given the opportunity and training, Negroes could do the same things as white men. Byrd's average score for the 25 weeks of training was 87.25 out of 100.00. This included diving physics, decompression tables, and first aid. So Walton concluded he would have to falsify the results of the tests in order to prevent Byrd from passing the course.

Walton was the first to break away from the stare. He looked over at the dressers, Williams and Smith, two young white males who admired him. Each diver was assigned two dressers and one tender. Dressers aided the diver in putting on the Mark V suit. Tenders made sure the diver's air lines did not become entangled. Normally, one of the dressers also would be the tender. Divers always had to be in a state of readiness. Their assigned roles in regards to a mission were interchangeable. They worked together like a machine. They had no choice. It was a matter of life and death. Each one had to trust and believe in all the other members of the team.

Chiefs have to make tough choices. This one was clearly the toughest in Walton's 22- year career. He chose to do the right thing. He elected to be an example to his men. It was his turn to take one for the team.

The Navy needed divers, and it did not matter whether they were Negro or white. What mattered was that they were willing and able to excel at their job. He could not in good conscience fail Byrd. He must always remain focused on the mission at hand. He belted out orders to Williams and Smith to dress the diver, and he quietly cursed the day he put his signature on those enlistment papers.

Walton's voice snapped Byrd out of the stare. He shook his head from side to side as if he had just awakened from a dream. He did not know what to call it. It was the first time he had experienced anything like this. His entire childhood had flashed before him in a matter of seconds, 57 seconds to be exact. Divers are trained to time everything. They develop an internal clock that becomes their lifeline. Quite often, whether or not they live to see another day is determined by their sense of timing. Dependent on air from the surface, deep sea divers must strategically time every mission. Enough time must be allotted to complete the assignment and return topside with sufficient air. During that period he saw his siblings. His only sister Ernestine, and remembered how she tenderly cared for him, because he was the youngest. Henry, who was second in line, was the sober-minded one. He never shied away from his responsibility to help their mom, or to keep him and his other two brothers in line, even though he was the shortest. He saw flashes of his brother Albert, who made them laugh until they cried with his clown-like behavior and jokes. Ned who was four years older than Sherman was the business-minded one.[58]Completing this final dive not only would be a dream come true for him but also would be a tribute to his siblings. All three of his brothers joined the Army during World War II and sent money home to his mother so that he could go to school.

As his mind drifted back to his family, his mother consumed most of his thoughts, as he was about to accomplish something she had made him believe he could do. Byrd recognized that his work ethic and his strict attention to detail came from her. She was a hard worker. Annie Lloyd had high hopes for all of her children. She believed each generation should strive for a better way of life, both in service to God and physical possessions. She encouraged them to dream big, work hard, and learn something new every day. Byrd was committed to doing just that.

He knew he was made for life at sea. He was engineered to feel at home in the water. Those times that he spent at the river with his brothers as a young child prepared him for the career he would have as an adult. Byrd remembered his last year at Stone Street High School. The teachers there would not let him hide behind excuses as to why he could not do something. They demanded that he execute all things in a spirit of excellence. These teachings fed into his competitive spirit. He loved to win, and he would not take a loss lying down. His displeasure of losing drove him to try to master everything he put his hands to, practicing over and over again until he became proficient.

A chill ran up his spine. His grandmother Mary Alice had once told him, "Son, if you ever see your life flash before you, it is a sign that you are getting ready to die. You will not have time to do or say much, but if you call Him, He will answer." She was talking about Jesus, her Savior, and Lord. Byrd quietly mumbled, "Jesus," but his spirit continued to utter much more. He reeled his mind back in like a fish caught on a line. Walton had given the order for him to prepare to dive.

Byrd was mindful that it was now his moment. He had proven to Walton and his classmates that he had a work ethic that was worthy of making him a brother. His sense of loyalty to those who initially hated him and wished him gone was overwhelming.

As he looked at his dressers, Williams and Smith, he could sense that their hatred for him had dissipated. Inwardly, he breathed a sigh of relief. He was about to make his final dive and being relaxed was an absolute must. Much of the anxiety Byrd felt on his way to the diving rig was now gone, and he was able to focus on the mission.

The mission required strategic use of his time. That meant he had no time for apprehension or alarm. Walton's capacity to successfully persuade the other deep sea diver candidates to accept Byrd into the brotherhood was a credit to his leadership abilities. After all, he was the chief.

As Williams and Smith began to dress him out, Byrd could not help but think about how significant this event would be. Although Negroes had a long way to go, their influence had started to pick up steam. Byrd was on the ground floor of desegregation in the military. During this period, Byrd's willingness to stand against the blatant and ruthless opposition of whites in the Navy put him in a position to affect change. Although it was not widespread at the time, Byrd could sense the change within the other deep sea diver students. He was encouraged. He had experienced a mutual respect among divers. Byrd knew who he was. No derogatory remarks or misdeeds could change that. He was a child of the King, and God's divine favor was upon him.

After a complete and thorough inspection of the Mark V diving suit, the dressers began to prepare Byrd for his final dive. They methodically worked together in the same manner as synchronized swimmers. Williams and Smith teamed up to assemble the diving suit on Byrd with respect due a qualified deep sea diver. It was an honor to put on his shoes. Williams doubled as the dive tender, ensuring that all the air hoses were untangled and in working order.

The Mark V deep sea diving suit weighed approximately 200 pounds. The watertight dress was 12 pounds, and each brass shoe weighed 17.5 pounds. The helmet weighed 54 pounds and the weighted belt, 84 pounds.[59]Byrd was now dressed and prepared to complete his final exercise. His future as a diver rested in God's hands, and he felt good. At this point, he was not worried. He was confident that the dressers had ensured that the diving suit was safe. He breathed quickly, smiled through the window of the helmet, and motioned that he was ready. With the helmeted Mark V MOD 1 now donned, Byrd was lowered into the water. He had just taken his final plunge off the diving rig as a student. The familiar chill of the water was refreshing.

When Byrd was raised out of the water back onto the diving rig, the sun was just about to set over the Anacostia River. Seeing the sunset metaphorically meant the close of a chapter in his life. He had executed the final test dive exercise with precision. So as a man practices so is he. Williams walked over and put his hand on Byrd's shoulder and said, "Congratulations my brother! You are now a United States Navy deep sea diver!" Then he and Smith bellowed out in unison, " Hooyah deep sea!"[60]

A few days later on April 4, 1955, Byrd graduated from the Deep Sea Divers C School in Class Number 2-55 as a First Class Diver.

IF MOMMA AIN'T HAPPY, AIN'T NOBODY HAPPY

Despite Sherman's great accomplishment, sadness hovered over the Christmas season that year. He had heard some of the older sailors say, "If momma ain't happy, ain't nobody happy." Shortly after Thanksgiving Day dinner in 1955, the truth of that statement hit home.

Weez was known to be a defender of the underdog. Any hint of children being mistreated infuriated her. Their home was a safe place for the neighborhood children to come and play. She always could find enough food to feed another mouth, even though her family was rapidly expanding.

Weez cooked large portions of food at every meal as if she were feeding 10 people instead of her family of five. One of the sailors or a neighbor may stop by, she would say. Often she would take a plate to the elderly woman who lived alone down the street. The extra food seldom was wasted, for Sherman loved leftovers.

But this year her heart was wounded, and it showed. In August Emmitt Till, a 14-year old boy from Chicago had been kidnapped, tortured and dumped in the Tallahatchie River in Mississippi. [61] The murder was horrific. It sent chills down the spine of Negro people across the nation.

Hatred and injustices continued. Many of these stories never reached the headlines of the local newspapers. What happened to Rosa Parks made the headlines. Mrs. Parks was arrested and put in jail for refusing to give up her seat on a bus in Montgomery, Alabama, to a white man on December 1, 1955. She was tired and so was Weez. Tired of the same-old promise that things were about to change. Weez felt helpless. She wanted to do something, but she did not know what. The Montgomery Improvement Association led by Martin Luther King knew exactly what to do. They organized a boycott of the Montgomery, Alabama, buses.[62]

Prolonged anger can turn to bitterness and Sherman did not want his wife to have lingering thoughts dampening her mood at Christmas. Their third child Azelle Carletha, nicknamed Nesa, turned one year old in November. Son Sherman Jr. was about to celebrate his third birthday on December 23. Weez had crying spells and often went to bed without eating. Sherman tried to comfort her, but she really grieved for the loss of innocent lives and feared for the safety of her own children. Weez was not her normal self and he needed to do what he could to help her get over this crossroad in her life. Ms. Irene thought that Weez could be experiencing the baby blues. She was six months pregnant with their fourth child. Her emotions seemed to be going haywire.

Sherman did not like the fact that many of these things seemed to be happening near his neck of the woods. He often calculated the probability of him making it out of Mississippi alive. According to his calculations, he only had a 40 percent chance. This was low. He was taking a huge risk remaining in the state where the Ku Klux Klan originated and thrived.

Sherman bowed his head and thanked God for giving his mother the desire and foresight to encourage her children to get as far away from Mississippi as possible. The newspaper had labeled it "The Great Migration." Negroes were leaving the cotton fields and relocating in the North, working industrial jobs. Owners of various factories were glad to receive the influx of cotton pickers. The southerners proved to be more productive than most people who grew up in the city. They were conditioned to working long hours without complaining. Wages were far greater than what was paid to them for working the cotton fields.[63]

Sherman held Weez in his arms every chance he got, praying every day that she would begin to feel better. He encouraged her to take it easy for a while. He cooked breakfast for every meal. The kids thought it was great. They did not have to eat any vegetables. Sherman cleaned up things around the house. The children were surviving. The situation reiterated his love and respect for all of the things Weez did on a daily basis. After the children fell asleep, he went straight to bed. He could not believe how exhausting it was to be a homemaker. Two weeks passed before Weez began to feel better.

Sherman could not put a finger on what had caused her to go through so many changes. He was just grateful that they had made the decision to move the whole family to Key West, Florida, while he was stationed on USS Petrel (ASR-14). It was his first assigned ship after completing Deep Sea Diver School. He knew that if they stuck together, with God's help, they could make it through all of the challenges life would throw their way.

CHAPTER NINE

EXPLOSIVE ORDNANCE DISPOSAL

Ayear had passed since Byrd was first assigned to *Petrel*, the Chanticleer-class submarine rescue ship. *Petrel* conducted variations of training exercises with Submarine Squadron 4 (SUBRON 4–CSS 4) in Key West, Florida. SUBRON 4 was a squadron of submarines based out of the U.S. Submarine Base in Pearl Harbor. The squadron began operations in Key West as a part of the Atlantic Fleet.

In 1956, Byrd was one of the divers who played a key role in freeing *USS Nantahala* (AO 60), the Ashtabula-class oiler that ran aground in the Key West Channel. Nantahala replenished 96 ships during the Suez Crisis, serving as the only fleet oiler in the Eastern Mediterranean.[64] Byrd was gaining a great deal of experience, and he was becoming more confident with each dive.

Working aboard *Petrel* was a deep sea diver's dream. The ship and crew stayed busy responding to various critical assignments. Living in Key West placed Byrd right in the thick of things. Key West was the home of the Underwater Swimmers School. This was the place where Underwater Demolition Team (UDT) and Explosive Ordnance Disposal (EOD) divers were taught how to use self-contained breathing apparatus (SCUBA).[65]

UDT assisted amphibious landings by investigating and destroying obstacles placed on beaches by the enemy. EOD disarmed all types of explosives and rendered safe biological, chemical, and nuclear weapons. UDT and EOD divers were combat swimmers.

These divers attended the same classes and graduated together from Underwater Swimmers School. Divers were no longer dependent on air from the surface, but rather they carried their air supply on their back in cylinders. Successful completion of SCUBA Diving School was a prerequisite for attendance at EOD School. Byrd was coming up on three years of experience as a deep sea diver and the natural progression of things would be to continue to be trained in UDT or EOD.

Byrd volunteered to become an EOD diver. EOD is arguably the most dangerous job in the U.S. Armed Forces. To achieve this goal he first would have to pass the Underwater Swimmers Class. The Navy's SCUBA diving course was taught in Key West. The Underwater Swimmers Class was five weeks long and entailed a minimum of 30 hours a week of classroom training. Byrd had to successfully pass courses in first aid, safety precautions, accident prevention, diving physics, and primary and secondary effects of pressure on the body. Students then had to master the characteristics, maintenance, and use of open-circuit, closed circuit, and semi-closed circuit types of SCUBA.[66]This was quite a feat for a Negro who was marked as unintelligent and unable to comprehend math and science. Byrd was not able to participate in any civil rights marches or freedom bus rides. Therefore to advance equal rights in the military, he studied fervently and practiced combat moves and diving drills until his body was completely exhausted. He was determined to quietly fight his present-day battles of prejudices so that Negro sailors who enlisted after him would know that they could achieve any rate, rating, or rank. Byrd knew where his help was coming from. All of his help was coming from the Lord.

Instructors paired this training with an adequate amount of time in the water to empower each student to accomplish missions at a depth of 100 feet and swim underwater for distances varying from 1 to 1,000 yards. Students trained using open- circuit air demand, such as the Aqua Lung, Northill Air Lung, and Scott Hydro-Pak.[67]Enlisted sailors had to be no older than 31 years of age to enroll in the five-week course. Although the training set no rating or pay grade limitations, ratings that aligned with EOD, UDT, and deep sea diving were highly recommended. Boatswain's mate fit right into this recommendation.[68]

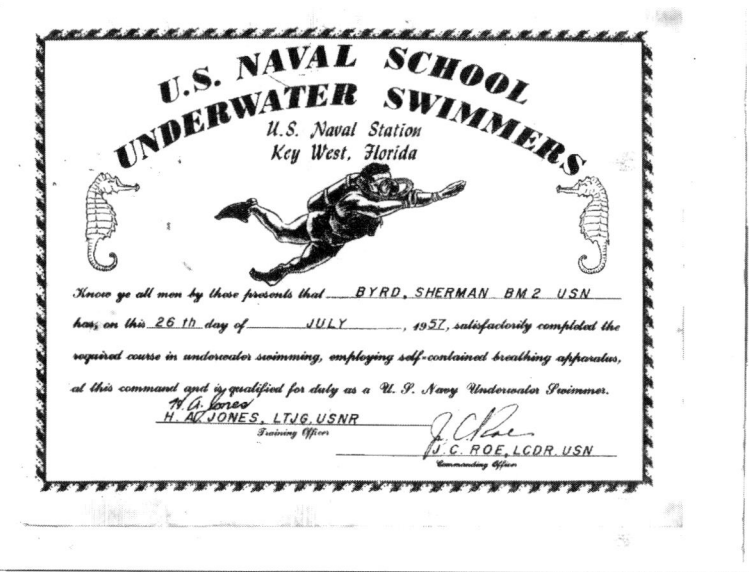

U.S. Naval School of Underwater Swimmers
Certificate Courtesy of the Byrd Family

NOT ONE BUT TWO

Much of what is accomplished by chiefs is not written down in any book. Information is passed down verbally from one chief to another or is admirably demonstrated. A chief's thoughts of his petty officers and enlisted men do not stop at 4:00 p.m. each day. They continue through the night. If they can help one of their sailors along the way, they gladly will do it. If they can give a little advice on life that may curtail future issues, chiefs will not hesitate to give it. So it was with Boatswain's Mate Chief Kenneth Calloway, Byrd's diving chief on Petrel.

Key West was quite the festive town. The year-round warm climate gave people a reason to celebrate the outdoors. Fishing, swimming, and riding bicycles were popular activities. Weez loved the outdoors and the carefree attitude of the people born in Key West. It appeared that no one in Key West was ever in a rush to do anything. Even the chickens that casually roamed the streets of the city could attest to that. There was nothing to worry about. Everything was going to be all right.

That is what Sherman found himself saying to Weez over and over again, as they each cuddled a bouncing baby girl early in the morning of October 2, 1957. Their quiver full of arrows instantly jumped from four children to six. What a surprise! As the doctor delivered the first baby girl at 5:10 a.m., he softly instructed Weez to keep pushing because another baby was right behind her. Four minutes later the second child was born. Sherman and Weez were now the shocked and proud parents of two healthy baby girls. The doctor also was shocked. Throughout the nine-month pregnancy he had heard only one heartbeat. Weez was larger than normal, but they were expecting a 9- or 10- pound boy. Word spread around the hospital like wildfire. The Naval Hospital in Key West had a set of twins onboard. Many people never had seen a set of twins. Sherman and Weez had picked out the name Andre if the baby was a boy, and Laurie Ann if it was a girl, in honor of his mother Annie Lloyd. Now neither of those names would work. So the quest for names began. Neighbors, friends, patients, and nurses all chimed in with suggested names. Weez was so overwhelmed by the reality of giving birth to twins, she hardly could think of any names that matched. Finally, the day after the birth of the twins, a nurse came in with a suggestion from an elderly woman who was a patient at the hospital. She suggested Cynthia and Sandra, and to call them Cindy and Sandy for short. Weez and Sherman loved this idea. Settling on names for the twins was a relief. Weez started planning a strategy to care for three little ones in diapers. Their fourth child Yolanda, whom they called Yo-Yo was only 18 months old.

Calloway and his wife Betty went to visit Byrd and Weez at the hospital. They bought gifts for the twins. As Betty and Weez admired every little move the twins made, Calloway pulled Sherman out into the hallway where they could talk privately. "Is there anything I can do for you?" asked Calloway. Byrd thought about it for a few seconds and said, "No, I cannot think of anything right now. Being the father of a set of twins is still somewhat of a shock! I am so happy that the three of them, Weez and the twins, are all healthy and doing fine. If I think of something, I will let you know." Calloway explained to Byrd that he understood how much of a shock that it must be to have two newborn babies instead of one.

"This might be a good time for you to get a vasectomy", said Calloway. "Doctors have compiled 30 years of research and data on operative patients attesting to the fact that there were no delayed adverse effects." Calloway, who on numerous other occasions had verbally challenged many of young lads who wanted to get married after their first sexual encounter, knew he had to take a kinder approach with Byrd. Weez and Sherman were happily married, and they loved each other very much. Calloway continued, "If you are going to reach your goal of being an explosive ordnance disposal diver, I need you to consider three things. First, you will have to obtain a top secret clearance. Your credit rating will have to be excellent. Additional children equal more money needed to care for them. This could lead to increased debt, which can easily turn into bad credit.

Second, you need to think about Louise and what these multiple pregnancies are doing to her body. Last but not least, college tuitions are increasing every year. You already have to save money for six children to go college, adding any more to that number would be absurd! EOD is an intense and prolonged sea-duty billet. That is a lot of responsibility for Weez to handle alone."

Byrd calmly listened to everything Calloway had to say. He concluded that it was the right conversation for them to have, but the timing was wrong. "Chief, I grew up without the provision and protection of my father. I am committed to do everything I possibly can to make sure my children will not go through the same thing. God has blessed Weez and me to have six wonderful children. I believe He will bless us to take care of them. I will do some research on vasectomy and talk to Weez about it when the time is right. Which road will we take? I don't know. One thing is for certain, I will surely bring the topic to the kitchen table. The kitchen table is where we make the bulk of our family decisions, usually over a late-night snack. God is faithful chief. Everything is going to be alright", said Byrd. He appreciated the fact that his chief did not shy away from talking to him about such a personal and delicate topic. Chiefs wear multiple hats. They must boldly approach their junior sailors with their concerns and in turn be easy to approach.[69]

EXPLOSIVE ORDNANCE DISPOSAL SCHOOL (EOD)

U.S. Navy EOD units have always played a critical role in warfare. They often have operated alongside special operations forces from all branches of the military. Trained to parachute jump, dive, and shoot, EOD are highly skilled combat swimmers. Since World War II, EOD units have deployed throughout the Mediterranean and the Pacific. These units, initially called Mobile Explosive Investigative Units (MEIU), were highly effective in performing one of the most dangerous jobs on land and at sea: clearing explosives.

The first class for EOD was in June 1941. The school originally was named Mine Recovery School and was located in Washington, D.C. Officers and enlisted personnel qualified as mine recovery personnel/second class divers after graduating from the ordnance school, which lasted 11 weeks.

Because of the ongoing conflict of the Korean War, and the explosive hazards left in its wake, the use of ordnance units had increased and the name changed from MEIU to EOD Units.

The EOD command was located on Jackson Road in Indian Head, Maryland, and had become the training center for explosive ordnances in 1946. The original schools were named the U.S. Navy Mine and Bomb Disposal Schools, which were combined and located at the Bellevue Annex of the Naval Gun Factory, where they had been since 1942. When the schools relocated to the Naval Powder Factory on Jackson Road, the training course was designated as EOD. [70]

EOD technicians were on call to respond to any type of ordnance. They received specialized training on how to handle explosives, which included U.S. and foreign mines. Trained to detonate and demolish hazardous munitions, they supported the fleet by removing mines from waterways. Duties also included assisting the Secret Service in the protection of the president, vice president, and other dignitaries of the United States.

BM2 Sherman Byrd arrived at Indian Head, Maryland, on December 5, 1957, ready to train at U.S. Naval School, Explosive Ordnance Disposal (NAVSCOLEOD). His reputation preceded him. Labeled a perfectionist, Byrd had earned the respect of those who worked with him. EOD was one of the career fields in which being a perfectionist was highly desired. The walls of discrimination were crumbling. This level of training required total trust in each member of the team, and the brotherly camaraderie had to be genuine. Byrd felt a peace about being there. He belonged at EOD because God had planned for him to be there.

The question in most people's mind was no longer whether a Negro was intelligent enough to be a diver. The question now was whether Byrd could handle the pressure. Death stood waiting at every corner. As a boatswain's mate, Byrd had become familiar with the many dangers of deck seamanship. In his opinion, danger was danger, whether it was attempting to diffuse a bomb or the handling of stores while replenishing at sea. In either case, a service member could lose his life. Byrd knew he was capable of performing the job with proper training. Dangerous missions required rigorous training and instruction. His classmates had nothing to worry about when it came to Byrd putting in his due. He was determined to give his all in his quest to become EOD qualified. He believed God. Whatever God had in store for him, no man could withhold from him.

Before the start of training, EOD students were given the EOD Manual for review. The amount of reading required was unimaginable. The job of an EOD diver was to neutralize all threats in the form of explosives. In a matter of 12 weeks, Byrd would be in the thick of the most dangerous job in the military.

The course covered instructions in the location, handling, and disposal of all types of land and underwater explosive ordnance, including the detailed operation of their fuses and exploder mechanisms. Although the class would be filled with men from the Army, Air Force, Marine Corps, and Navy, only the men in the Navy would be trained in underwater ordnance.

Byrd did not care about the prestige that came along with being a part of an elite unit. God had given him purpose. His intent was to contribute to the greater good by risking his life to save others. He was there to support the mission: remove all threats to operations and personnel.

As more intense training approached, Byrd found himself gearing up to match it with an equal level of intensity. EOD drills tugged at Byrd's competitive nature. With every class and training exercise, Byrd brought his best effort.

The extreme nature of the EOD program was enough to wear anyone down. Mental and physical preparation was crucial. EOD was serious, and instructors cautiously put the students into the most stressful of situations. Wartime was not a walk through the park. Instructors in the EOD program made sure that each student knew it. The pressure applied was a deliberate test of each student's skill and sheer will. Having an understanding of the seriousness of the job was the difference between being blown to bits or coming home in one piece.

The harshness of this reality is symbolized by the EOD emblem "Junk in the Sun." This military emblem is duplicated throughout the Navy, Marine Corps, Army, and Air Force. These team members train together, day in and day out, coordinating their movements, interchanging roles as necessary. Uttering few words, these quiet professionals communicate through familiarity. Practice makes perfect. They understand the costs. With sober minds and steadfastness of heart, they volunteered to be a part of a sacrificial team, willing to die for their country. The "Junk" is the sea mine, torpedo, or Navy-standard missile. Whatever is displaced by the explosion of the Junk creates the "Junk in the Sun." [71]

EOD's official motto Per Scientiam Servitia epitomizes, "Service through Knowledge". [72] Approximately 20 different countries made land mines, including France, Germany, England, and China, just to name a few. EOD divers are trained to identify various architectures. Brand name, year made, and fuse type are pinpointed in a matter of seconds. Divers log 2,000 hours of study, familiarizing themselves with 24 technical manuals and topics such as marine biology, basic electronics, shark defense, and underwater first aid.

Each team of one officer and two enlisted men, transport 1,000 pounds of equipment, counter-explosives, and 400 tools. The assigned mission is to locate, render safe, and recover highly explosive sea mines, torpedoes, and standard missiles found on land or in the sea. [73]

The unofficial motto of the emblem "Junk in the Sun" is "Initial Success or Total Failure." [74]

"INITIAL SUCCESS OR TOTAL FAILURE"

Junk in the Sun
Reproduction Courtesy of Charles Collins III

The weight of this truth rests in the souls of each person on the team. Every day, they make a conscious decision to commit to succeed. These volunteers are well aware of the calculated and uncalculated risks they are taking, and yet they press on toward perfection.

Fieldwork required focus. The last thing the military needed were EOD techs overwhelmed by distractions. One distraction was a signed death certificate. It also was possible that accidents could occur. The Indian Head command experienced this reality on December 18, 1957.

Less than two weeks after Byrd's arrival, he quickly learned the critical nature of his job. NAVSCOLEOD lost two of its students. While on a training mission, a proximity fuse from a M103 bomb was fully functional at the time a young Army Private Matthew Conway picked it up. The bomb exploded, killing Conway and Airman Second Class Nathaniel Stone. EOD students trained with live ammunitions. The EOD community mourned the loss of their two brothers. Conway and Stone were in their early twenties.[75]Death had no age limit.

Byrd recognized the need to pause for a moment and pay respect to the families of the fallen warriors, so, too, did the entire command. The command encouraged the students to do something that would de-stress them from the rigorous apprenticeship. Clarity of mind was an absolute must in EOD training. De-stressing had to be within the limits.

Byrd found it was helpful to take a swim. It did not matter if it was an ocean or a pool, swimming relieved stress in his body and mind. Another avenue to de-stress was watching a game of football. His favorite college player out of Syracuse was drafted into the NFL by the Cleveland Browns, running back Jim Brown. Byrd believed Brown was the best player who came out of college even though he was drafted as the sixth pick.

When he was not checking the stats on his favorite football player, Byrd was voraciously studying his EOD Manual. On base, that was Byrd's claim to fame. He was known as Mr. Attention-to-Detail, receiving a score of SAT consistently. The high marks in his service record were no flukes, and he maintained an elevated level of professionalism. He brought this same level of intensity to extracurricular activities, including pickup football and volleyball games. He was a fierce competitor. Fiery competition away from class gave Byrd the balance he needed.

Early in his EOD training, Byrd took the lead and cultivated camaraderie. His shipboard training had kicked in. As a boatswain's mate, Byrd had learned a great while ago that he had to develop himself as a leader. On the ship, he was responsible for the overall job, and not just a segment of it. He learned that he was responsible for the safety and well- being of his crew. He applied this same mentality to his EOD training. On June 6, 1958, Byrd successfully graduated from NAVSCOLEOD. He was grateful to God for keeping him safe from hurt, harm and danger.

Explosive Ordnance Disposal Class 04B-58
Photo Courtesy of the United States Navy

Graduates of NAVSCOLEOD are screened for further advanced training. Knowledge and perfectly executed missions were top priorities for the continuation of training in nuclear weapons disposal. On June 9, 1958, Byrd entered Special Weapons Disposal School. Details of the six-weeks of training remained top secret. During this course Byrd's unit lost another student, GM1 Steele. This time an explosion was not the cause. One of the worst things that a combat swimmer can hear is his chief or unit officer say in front of the panel, "Sirs, I do not care to work with him in the field." If the chief or unit officer did not feel that a person could execute the mission 100 percent of the time, under every possible scenario, they were obligated to look out for the other team members who would be put at risk. It was better to let one student go, than to lose two or three on a mission. This happened to GM1 Steele, and he was dropped from the Special Weapons Disposal School. After satisfactorily completing all facets of the training course, Byrd graduated with Class Number 29-58SWD.

CHAPTER TEN

QUIET STRONG

On July 25, 1958, Byrd transferred to *USS Randolph* (CVA-15), the Ticonderoga Essex-class attack aircraft carrier, to serve in an EOD diver billet. Soon after graduation, he began to fulfill temporarily assigned duties assisting the U.S. Secret Service in the protection of the president of the United States. Byrd was humbled and honored to be chosen to serve his country in this manner. This was a game-changing accomplishment. The U.S. government believed he could be trusted. A Negro from the cotton fields of Mississippi had the integrity, professionalism, and knowledge to be a part of their team. Byrd rejoiced in this victory.

This was a top-secret assignment. Nobody had to know. Byrd was quiet. Byrd was strong.

Fortunately, Byrd was not the only one moving and shaking up things en route to achieving his own personal career goals. A 1958 Amendment to the Career Compensation Act of 1949 created the U.S. Navy pay grades for E-8 senior chief and E-9 master chief. Examinations for the quickly labeled "Super Chiefs" were held on August 5, 1958. Byrd was ecstatic to find out that Chief Walton from Deep Sea Divers School was advanced from E-7 to E-9. It had taken a real act of courage for Walton to maintain his integrity while Byrd navigated through Deep Sea Divers School. Byrd committed to emulate Walton when he became a chief. He would never forget all the things he learned under his leadership. Walton consistently set a good example for his men to follow.

A few months after his arrival aboard *Randolph*, Byrd had the pleasure of hearing an inspirational speech given by one of the greatest orators of the World War II era, Sir Winston Churchill. One of the boatswain's mates had the privilege of piping the arrival of the British prime minister on October 26, 1958.[76] The boatswain's pipe has long been a pillar of the Navy's tradition. Byrd was intrigued by the honored guest. He was impressed by Churchill's ability to influence people and governments. When Churchill departed from *Randolph*, most sailors aboard felt charged and prepared to accomplish greater things. Byrd was one of those sailors. He silently made a commitment to himself to go back to school and complete his high school diploma.

FIDEL CASTRO

On New Year's Day 1959, news hit the airwaves that a young Cuban nationalist, Fidel Castro, invaded Havana and overthrew Dictator General Fulgencio Batista, the nation's president. Havana, as well as other parts of Cuba, began celebrating their future. In the eyes of most Cubans, Castro was a revolutionary, a messiah.

Batista was backed and supported by the U.S. government. He spearheaded two political coups that empowered him to govern Cuba on two separate occasions. In 1933, as the self-appointed chief of the military, he became a favored U.S. strong man when he toppled the liberal government of Gerardo Machado. The first coup made him the authority in Cuba, which was confirmed by the support of the U.S. Ambassador Benjamin Sumner Welles, who put extreme pressure on Machado to relinquish his authority in favor of an administration Batista would oversee.

After losing control in 1944, Batista took over the Cuban government for the second time on March 10, 1952, gaining formal support from U.S. President Dwight D. Eisenhower. The Cuban government under Batista was good for American business. However, organized crime and large-scale gambling in Havana, enterprises that made Batista rich, caused many to fear and question the new Cuban government.[77]

Young Fidel Castro eased many of those fears when he ousted Batista. This occurred after his first attempt to overthrow Batista at the Moncada Army Barracks in 1953 miserably failed. His attack landed him in jail and provoked what came to be known as the "ten-for-one" law. Batista ordered that 10 rebels be murdered for every soldier who was killed, which eventually resulted in the death of 59 rebels.[78]

U.S. corporations secured profitable contracts with Cuba while Batista reigned. After Castro was released from jail in 1955, anti-Batista rallies and riots amplified. At this point, Castro had gained loyalty and support from the Cuban population. Batista had not put in place any nationwide program for the betterment of the Cuban people, a fact that Castro emphasized in his four-hour manifesto entitled "History Will Absolve Me." Castro was a sharp lawyer, and his speech was considered to be the early declaration of the Cuban Revolution. When the story of Castro's invasion broke, *Randolph* was in the Atlantic Ocean with the Sixth Fleet heading to the Mediterranean Sea and Lebanon. The ship already had been deployed to GTMO on three different occasions. Crewmembers, as well as every other American it seemed, knew that Castro's invasion into Havana could turn into a crisis.[79]

Randolph continued its operations in the Mediterranean Sea, and the Castro incident continued to heighten. Trouble was brewing south of Miami. The Cubans were thrilled with their new leader. American officials did not share the same enthusiasm. Byrd discerned that the swing of power down in Cuba could have a drastic effect on the U.S. economy.

Upon hearing about Castro's rise to power and the removal of Batista, Byrd could not escape the gnawing feeling that Castro's invasion of Havana was only the start. The United States would take action. Too much was at stake. He knew that Castro disapproved of America's approach to business and interests in Cuba. With Castro in power, it would only be a matter of time before Cuba posed an enormous threat to American interests. The tense situation between the United States and Cuba had begun to reach a boiling point. Many wealthy Cubans fled to the United States and joined with the Central Intelligence Agency (CIA) in trying to push Castro from power. [80]

The Containment Strategy initiated by the Truman administration was crucial. It needed to be protected at all costs. President Eisenhower had a one-track mind concerning Communism. He would protect America's economic interests at all costs, which included invading Cuba when the time was ripe. Byrd had mixed feelings concerning everything that had been happening. In his opinion, the system of Communist regimes was wrong on so many levels. He applauded Eisenhower's efforts to eradicate its expansion. Nevertheless, capitalism, the system that had become the framework of America, did not benefit Negroes. Jim Crow was still alive and well.

USS *Independence* (CVA-62) was commissioned on January 10, 1959, and was the last ship in the Forrestal class of attack aircraft carriers. When Byrd arrived on April 16, 1959, the *Independence* was operating off the Virginia Capes doing training maneuvers.

Byrd was at a brand-new duty station on a brand-new ship. What he experienced in his short six-month stay was far from unfamiliar. No matter where he went, he could not escape his complexion. His rating and reputation continued to frighten an anger most of the white shipmates outside of his EOD team. Frustrated over the milestones Byrd had achieved, they would carefully watch what he was doing most of the day. They were in search of a time when they could catch him by himself. Then they could tell him how they really felt and no one else would hear. People he did not even know. Such was the case early one morning as he was relieved of standing duty. As he headed to his bunk to get some sleep, a white ship-mate stopped him and said, "Hey Byrd, you ain't nothing but the Navy's guinea pig. Some freak experiment to see how much your body and mind can take. You are just a fly in a cup of milk! Sooner or later you are going to drown!" Byrd stopped dead in his tracks. He turned to face his shipmate, only to see him running away. He was a Gunner's Mate, E-4. Many sailors did not want to acknowledge Byrd as a person of higher rate. They refused to give him the respect he deserved. As he walked away he could feel the anger rising up in him. There was no way he could go to sleep now! Here was a man who hated him so much that he wanted him to drown. He took no thought of how hard Byrd's death would be on his wife or his children! Byrd had never seen him before. How many more people on the ship felt the same way? His words were like a sucker punch! He said it and ran away. Some days Byrd grew tired of the same old prejudices. It would pop up so unexpectedly, from out of nowhere! He went up to the main deck and travelled back to the stern of the ship. He gazed out at the water and prayed to Almighty God. The water always had a calming effect on him. He asked God for strength to complete his journey. Fame and fortune was not what he sought, he yearned to do the will of God. As he thought about what the white sailor had said, Byrd decided to use the analogy for motivation. The sailor was right. He was a fly in a cup of milk. The blackness of his skin boldly stood out amidst the sea of his white shipmates. Yet he was wrong about him drowning. He was not going to drown! The fly had a few options.

Byrd encouraged his own self, and hollered out, "Sink or swim Byrd, sink or swim!" Byrd chose to swim! It was as if a light clicked on in his head. God had been preparing him to go through these trials years ago! His brothers had taught him how to endure. They continually threw him back into the Tallahatchie River until he learned how to swim. If the fly could keep swimming until he reached the inward edge of the cup, he could slowly grip one leg onto the dry surface and begin to climb out. It would not be easy, but it could be done! Byrd knew that God could make a way out of no way, and he would trust Him to do just that! Right then and there, Byrd renewed his vow to keep his hand in the hand of the Man that stills the water. Sink or swim would become his new battle cry! From here on out, whenever the hatred seemed unbearable, he would rejoice in the fact that he was just a fly in a cup of milk! God had gifted him with the ability to swim! He was an expert. Surely, he could complete his God-given assignment. He would endure to the end!

In contrast to his treatment by some of the shipmates on the *Independence*, the brotherly bond between Byrd and his EOD team was real. They completely trusted one another with their life. In fact, at the culmination of his EOD training, the chief stood before the EOD officer and made a declaration saying, "I do care to work with Boatswain's Mate Second Class Sherman Byrd in the field." This statement confirmed his acceptance as an EOD diver. Hearing the chief confirm his confidence in Byrd's knowledge, skills, and abilities generated a joy he was not able to describe. Confirmation from the same chief who had drilled him daily, the same chief who had pushed him to his breaking point, and when he did not break, pushed him some more. EOD was a brotherhood and without hesitation Byrd was accepted into the fold. As a member of his EOD team once said, "It is extremely difficult to hate the person disarming the bomb right next to you. In light of the crisis at hand, who cares about the color of his skin?"

THE BAY OF PIGS

Fidel Castro's regime had become even more of a threat to America's interests. He immediately took steps to reduce American influence on the island. At the height of the conflict the Eisenhower administration cut off sugar imports from Cuba. Soon after, the Soviet Union agreed to buy that sugar. The sugar and oil deal was signed when Soviet Deputy Prime Minister Anastas Mikoyan visited Cuba in February 1960. The new agreement would keep the Cuban economy from collapsing. Early on, the American government did not know exactly what to think of Castro. They had not weighed the Cuban problem too heavily in light of the struggles of the Cold War. It soon became evident however, that Communist influence had become the motivating factor for Castro.[81]

The administration must have known that Cuba would take the next step in squeezing the American agenda. Cuba nationalized U.S.-owned oil refineries after the U.S. refused to process oil provided by the Soviet Union. Fidel Castro continued to threaten U.S. businesses, and he continued to have a major negative effect on the entire U.S. political system. Castro marched closely with the Communist block and seized almost all of the U.S. property in Cuba.

During this tense time of the two countries playing cat and mouse, Byrd mentally and physically prepared himself for conflict. As a boatswain's mate, Byrd was all too familiar with the dangers of built-up strain on mooring lines. If a mooring line were to snap under heavy strain, it could seriously injure a sailor and perhaps even kill him.

On a more personal level, another situation had crept into the mix for Byrd. He was in position to advance to boatswain's mate first class. He had passed all the necessary examinations with very high scores. In fact, Byrd had high marks in every training class he took since joining the Navy. His chain of command could not deny that Byrd was an outstanding EOD diver, and an even better student. With the exception of Captain's Mast, which did not result in suspension of duty, Byrd's service record was exemplary.

The Navy diver ratings carried an extensive sea-duty obligation. Byrd took that into consideration before ever volunteering. Twelve years after joining the Navy, Byrd was assigned shore duty at Naval Ammunition and Net Depot (NAND), Seal Beach, California. After being onboard approximately seven months, Byrd was advanced to Boatswain's Mate First Class.

Two months later, July 1960, Byrd satisfactorily passed the United States Armed Forces Institute's high school level General Educational Development Tests (GED). In Byrd's mind, receiving his GED was one of the most monumental things he had ever accomplished. In spite of all the in-depth technical manuals he had to familiarize himself with, completing his high school education brought a gratification never before experienced. Byrd wanted to be able to encourage his children to complete their high school education, so he knew that he must complete his first. Winston Churchill encouraged him to take things to a higher level, and he did! No one could ever take his diploma away. It was his forever. Byrd took a deep breath. He was happy! Relations between the United States and Cuba continued to mount. Adding to the dilemma was Castro's visit with Nation of Islam minister, Malcolm X at the Hotel Theresa. The rendezvous took place on September 24, 1960, two days before Castro's speech at the United Nations. When Castro met with Malcolm X at the Hotel Theresa, he played the political card almost to perfection. Eisenhower already had snubbed him by failing to invite Castro to a parade and reception in Midtown for Latin American leaders. Castro was incredibly smart and resourceful. He used Eisenhower's snub to his advantage. He responded by inviting the poor Negro people of Harlem to the Hotel Theresa for a luncheon that he sponsored. The gesture made the Cuban leader all the more popular. In the eyes of those slighted by the capitalist U.S. government, it added more weight to Castro's cause. He was a freedom fighter.[82]

Castro and U.S.–Cuban relations were not the only issues of concern on Byrd's mind. It was a tense global situation. The crises paralleled the 1960 presidential campaign. Stopping the spread of Communism in the Western Hemisphere was one of the more pressing issues. Now that Castro was in power, the reality of Cuba becoming a Communist regime was inevitable. Whoever followed President Eisenhower would have to make every effort to eradicate it.

Because Byrd was an EOD professional, he forced himself to suppress his personal feelings about the right presidential candidate. Focusing his mind on the U.S. Navy EOD mission helped him to compartmentalize. His mission was to support national security strategies that included detecting explosive ordnances on land and under water.

Another critical part of his mission was to work alongside Secret Service to protect the president of the United States.

Just as he had worked to protect President Eisenhower, he would do the same for the next president whether he was a Democrat or a Republican. Alongside Castro's regime, the Soviet influence, and the run for office was a serious domestic dilemma. The nation was deeply divided. Civil unrest was prominent. Negroes demanded equal rights and their votes could very well be the deciding factor in the upcoming presidential election. Byrd took his EOD responsibilities seriously. It was important to him to carry out his duties while maintaining his personal integrity. He would exercise his right to vote. Too many people died throughout the struggle of the civil rights movement to afford him this opportunity. His choice for president would not interfere with his commitment to serve in the capacity of an EOD diver.

Vice President Richard Nixon favored military intervention of Cuba. President Eisenhower opposed it. Castro's ties to the Soviet Union had provoked the president to authorize the CIA to train and equip 1,400 Cuban exiles, known as Brigade 2506. The exiles initiated a counterrevolution to overthrow Castro. The mission was labeled the Bay of Pigs. The designated location of attack was on the south central side of Cuba. Brigade 2506 fled Cuba when Fidel Castro ousted General Fulgencio Batista from power. The exiles lived in Miami, Florida, and trained in Guatemala.

President Eisenhower broke diplomatic ties with Cuba in January 1961. This was one of his final acts as president. This invasion could mark the beginning of World War III. Newly elected President John F. Kennedy was hesitant to proceed. He agreed to move forward with the invasion if America's support of the attack would not be revealed. On April 15, 1961, an air attack of Cuba was launched. The goal was to destroy the limited Cuban air force. A U.S. land attack would follow two days later.

The Bay of Pigs invasion failed. Castro's military intelligence knew of the planned attack. Their counterattack forced the Cuban exiles to surrender within 24 hours. The botched invasion brought immeasurable embarrassment to the United States and President Kennedy.[83]

CHAPTER ELEVEN

THE GOAT LOCKER IN THE CROSSHAIRS

At a time when Negroes in America found themselves in an intense struggle to obtain their civil rights and forge ahead on the American landscape, Byrd quietly battled the same issues in the military. He was cognizant of the fact that noncommissioned officers were the backbone of the U.S. Navy. In fact, noncommissioned officers were the backbone of the entire armed forces. Although Byrd advanced in rate, he found himself waist deep in the racial tension that still divided the fleet.

As was his custom, Byrd began to research the history of the Chief Petty Officer (CPO). Research of history, and practical application were all part of Byrd's personality. This made him a viable candidate for any position he sought, especially chief. At each point in his career thus far, Byrd showed that he was both a leader and a technical expert. He was awarded four Good Conduct Medals from four different duty stations.

Byrd continued to work on his craft and fine-tuned his leadership skills. He took the initiative to teach junior sailors about seamanship and boatswain's mate skills. Being a boatswain's mate, he was in the perfect rating to exhibit his abilities. Even as a seaman apprentice (E-2), Byrd focused on passing all of his examinations on the first attempt. He was a leader on paper and on deck.

Byrd was betting that at some point in his career, he would be mentoring young future leaders in the Navy. He was a natural on the hunt for CPO because he enjoyed Navy life. He wanted to be able to affect change. Deep down inside, he was a teacher. Despite the animosity of racial tension that continued to brew nationwide, he developed close and respectful relationships at every duty station. It was no secret to the chain of command that Byrd would pursue the Goat Locker.

Negroes had begun to kick-start a new era in the history of the civil rights movement. When Byrd voiced his intent to become a CPO, it reinforced the notion that the race wars were on the rise again. Some in military service were in favor of his ambition, others were angered. Negroes seemed to be taking over.

If the Navy had not figured out that Byrd was a fighter by now, personnel became well aware once he made BM1. There would be no stopping him. The power of God was the wind beneath his sails. Byrd was a force to be reckoned with.

The rate of the CPO was established on April 1, 1893, and the earliest known use of the term dated back to 1776. Aboard *USS Alfred*, a cook's mate, Jacob Wasbie developed the moniker of Chief Cook. He was understood to be the foremost cook aboard the ship. [84]

The first Negro CPO was John Henry "Dick" Turpin. On June 1, 1917, Turpin became chief gunner's mate aboard *USS Marblehead*. He remained in that rate until he retired on October 5, 1925. [85]

Byrd heard rumors that becoming a Navy chief was nearly impossible. It was especially illogical for a Negro to desire the rate. Byrd's critics failed to recognize his expertise, sharp mental power, and spirit of servitude. He was an expert boatswain's mate and excelled at blocking out negativity. This was a character trait that every sailor needed to advance. He never lost sight of his dream. Byrd knew that having a dream to advance in rate would need to evolve into a plan. He eagerly began to make plans to don the uniform of CPO. For a senior enlisted position, Byrd would have to compete against a large group of first class petty officers. He was aware of the hidden challenges. His experiences over the years caused him to conclude that all men were equal. It was their personal choices and variant exposures to life that made them different.

He started his rigorous campaign by researching the history of the CPO Charge Book. The book was a collection of study material and comprehensive notes, which had to be perused en route to CPO initiation. In the late 1950s, initiations into the CPO community began to take place. He watched and kept track of some of the things done by the newest candidates for chief, often jotting down notes in his notepad for later study and personal practice.

The study of World War II dominated much of Byrd's leisure time and for numerous reasons. One reason was to confirm and to document the advancement protocol for future CPO. During World War II, commanding officers were authorized to advance deserving and qualified sailors to the highest enlisted rate of CPO. The determination of "deserving and qualified" could have been difficult for the commanding officer. The situation also presented challenges to the sailor who aspired to attain a chief's rating. How best to prepare? How to plan and track preparation? How to best display your qualifications? From these dilemmas sprang the original charge books. [86]

The information Byrd was able to obtain was valuable. At the time of the war, chiefs began to direct first class petty officers to prepare themselves to assume additional responsibilities by recording details of those duties. EOD Chief Kelly at Seal Beach confirmed Byrd's findings. A stickler for details, Byrd embraced the necessity to consistently document.

During his first deployment on *Tarawa*, Byrd often researched information in the ships professional library. The other ships he deployed on had limited resources. Ship's professional libraries generally were nonexistent or poorly stocked. Much had to be learned directly from conversations with the chiefs themselves and written down to be studied later. In addition to the technical aspects of the various ratings, CPOs also talked to the first class aspirants about leadership, accountability, supporting the chain of command, and other professional subject matter. Often, they used their personal experiences to illustrate how things should be done.

Becoming a chief in the world's finest navy would require Byrd to make moral and ethical decisions. On a smaller scale, Byrd recognized that achieving the rate of chief was still warfare. And he was wise enough to know that he had to make the right calculations to advance.

The madness of racial inequality still dominated the country. Byrd had no choice but to plan his work and work his plan. The goal was to "Be the Chief!" This goal should always be a young sailor's motivation for doing well and working hard. To meet this aim, the would-be CPO had to choose between two paths of behavior: selfless or self-serving.

The selfless path required putting self aside, taking the hard tours, and going where the Navy needed him. Byrd had to satisfy mission objectives at all costs, regardless of the time required to complete the task. The self-serving path forced one to fake positive perceptions to keep images alive, just to earn high marks.

Most CPOs earned the right to wear the proud uniform. They chose a path on which the echo of "I" or "me" was inaudible. Chiefs invested numerous hours at their designated watch station, motivating, training, and counseling junior sailors.

Being a chief meant being thoroughly concerned about the welfare of their sailors. The term shipmate meant more than simply wearing the same Navy uniform. It meant being committed to the sailor standing next to you. It did not matter if they were Negro, white, or any other race. Chiefs ensured their sailors understood their commitment. It was the root idea of leadership.

Obtaining the rate of chief would be difficult, but Byrd was prepared to fight the uphill battle. Now that he was a petty officer first class, his chief would give him plenty of opportunities to lead morning musters, verify completion of work, and counsel those sailors who were junior to him. Byrd learned how to pick his battles wisely. He had the spirit to fight for his junior sailors.

KITCHEN TABLE DECISIONS

It was July 1961, and Sherman was assigned to NAND, Seal Beach, California. He was EOD trained, and his job was a little more dangerous than Weez had led the children to believe. All that they knew was their dad was a Navy diver, and he went swimming almost every day. Their children ranged in age from three to ten years old. It would be a long way down the road before they could understand the fact that their dad disarmed bombs. She and Sherman had agreed to cross that bridge when they got to it.

Weez was good about establishing a routine for the children to follow. Structure was a critical part of their daily lives. Her days started out with her and Sherman enjoying breakfast together. Nothing heavy, but something light. Oatmeal with nuts was his favorite. The kitchen table had always been a special place for them. They eagerly gathered there in the morning and evening to talk about the things that occurred each day. Sitting side by side, they often exchanged a kiss or two.

The children had completed another school year, and Weez and Sherman discussed how they fared. Education was a top priority to both of them. They wanted all of their children to complete high school and attend college. Weez turned toward Sherman and said, "I am a little worried about Shirley. She is ten years old, and she has passed on to the sixth grade. I am not so sure if we made the right decision years ago when we allowed her to start school a year early. We thought it was a good idea at the time. She began talking at a very young age. You and I were able to teach her many of the things that she needed to know to advance from kindergarten to first grade. She knew the alphabets, colors, and numbers up to 20 by the time she was five years old. When her kindergarten teacher suggested that we allow her to move up to the first grade, we thought it was a good idea. We evaluated the pros and cons and decided to allow her to reach her potential. What started out as a good idea, however, is not turning out the way we expected. Shirley can keep pace with the older students when it comes to the academic portion of the schoolwork, but her maturity level is clearly a year behind." "I agree," said Sherman. "She is still very much attached to you. She shies away from making friends and only has one or two. I think I had a lot to do with it. Shirley is our first born child. My love for her is unexplainable. I picked her up every chance I got, and almost everything she wanted, I gave it to her. In a lot of ways, I was trying to make up for the void of not being able to spend time with my dad because of his incarceration. I spoiled her. She is a daddy's girl. That is the bottom line," said Sherman. They both laughed for a brief moment. Weez and Sherman were not trying to make light of the situation. It was just great to have those moments when they could be completely themselves. She did not have to speak baby talk, and he was relieved of speaking technical jargon. They knew how to make each other smile. Weez said, "Well Shirley seems to be happy, but I wonder if she really is. Another concern I have is that year after year; she is the shortest person in her class. I wonder if she is being bullied by the older children." Sherman said, "Mrs. Cherry, her teacher, never mentioned anything about her being bullied at the Parent-Teacher Association meetings (PTA). I will call the school today. Hopefully I can get the principal to call Mrs. Cherry and ask her about it." They agreed to research possible remedies to the situation.

Sherman Jr. passed on to the third grade. His grades were above average, but he had trouble keeping still. He was an active child. Weez and Sherman decided to challenge him to be still while reading a book. They could increase the length of the books as he adjusted to the additional time that he was able to remain still. Hopefully, by the end of the summer, his ability to sit still and focus will have improved.

Nesa did well in kindergarten grade, and in September, she would be entering the first grade. She and Sherman Jr. were close in age, but they did not share the same interests. Nesa was a little princess in all aspects of the word. She did not like to get dirty, nor did she find any pleasure in breaking a sweat. She liked to go outside, but it was more for socializing than getting any exercise. Weez and Sherman decided to try to get her involved utilizing some different family outings that required exercise. They could go to the zoo or play a game of dodge ball. They often took the children to the beach. Nesa did not enjoy playing in the water as much as her siblings. She did not want the water to mess up her hair.

Yo-Yo was a force to be reckoned. The thinnest of all the children, she was hands down the most aggressive. Smart as a whip and fast as a cougar. She zoomed around the house hardly stopping to catch her breath. She was obedient enough to be still when directed, but when it was time to play she would be gone in seconds. Weez had taught her at home during the school year, and she was ready to attend kindergarten in September. The real question was if the teachers at the kindergarten were ready for her.

Last but not least, they discussed the twins, Cindy and Sandy. At the age of three, their distinct personalities were already prevalent. Sandy was the leader, and Cindy was the follower. Sandy was outgoing and into everything. Cindy was easy going and obedient. The more Weez and Sherman talked, the more they realized that the twins were tiny examples of them. Sandy was more like Weez. Cindy was more like Sherman (she even had his dimples). They looked at each other and laughed. God certainly had a sense of humor.

Weez and Sherman had their work cut out for them. Parenting was not for the lazy, neither for the faint of heart. They would tackle the children's various issues together, and bask in the joy that they brought them. Sherman got up from the table to go to work.

CHAPTER TWELVE

WHILE YOU WERE SLEEPING

The conversation still wreaking havoc in the locker room was the failed Bay of Pigs invasion. Several months had passed, but the wound was still fresh. Byrd elevated his training routines, for he understood that this was not the way the story would end. His time at NAND, Seal Beach, California, was filled with intense study and plenty of opportunities to execute what he had learned. The world of conventional, biological, chemical and nuclear weapons constantly changed. Many nations had capabilities to create weapons of mass destruction. His job was to render those weapons safe wherever found.

Such a call came in at 7:19 on Tuesday morning, October 3, 1961. Commander, Minecraft, U.S. Pacific Fleet requested EOD assistance in the recovery of a U.S. torpedo from Mexican territorial waters. The EOD's mission was to locate, render safe, and recover. The mission would be accomplished from USS Reaper (MSO 467), the aggressive Agile-class minesweeper, attained for the purpose of removing mines placed in water to prevent the passage of ships. A team was put together that included an EOD officer and two divers: Lieutenant Commander Turner, BMC (DV) P. A. Kelly, and BM1 (DV) Sherman Byrd.

Chiefs are subject matter experts. They are working supervisors, who lead by example. They often are called upon to take charge of the most dangerous and time-critical missions. Providers of on-the-job and classroom training, chiefs know the capabilities of each of their junior sailors.

Chief Kelly and Byrd were briefed on the situation. A strategy was devised. The mission began. "Byrd, you take the lead on this one," said Chief Kelly. "Roger that Chief," Byrd answered. Chiefs gauge the technical and professional progress of each of their junior sailors. They will increase the sailor's areas of responsibilities as warranted.

Reaper was standing by for their arrival. The half-ton of equipment was already packed, prepared, and waiting for the next mission. Time was critical, and whenever EOD was called upon, they launched quickly. Kelly and Byrd loaded the working toolbox onto the small boat. The three-man crew, Turner, Kelly, and Byrd, launched out.

Loose lips sink ships, and specifically for that reason, it was normal policy for the details of an EOD mission to be on a "need-to-know" basis aboard ship. So it was no surprise that while some of the *Reaper's* crew assisted the EOD team as they climbed the Jacob's ladder, other sailors scurried down below to inform their shipmates. As the sailors hurried to the main deck, many were shocked to see that the team included a Negro EOD diver. Few men, Negro or white, could successfully navigate the rigors of becoming EOD qualified. It meant a lot for a Negro to see someone like Byrd pass the physical and mental requirements to become a diver. Byrd remained focused and undeterred while the mission was at hand, only nodding his head to acknowledge the four Negro shipmates.

Reaper proceeded full speed ahead to the vicinity where the torpedo was lost in Mexican territorial waters. The area extended out three miles from the Mexican shore. It was a delicate situation and a difficult task. If the torpedo exploded, it could cause considerable damage to the people and land alongside the Mexican shoreline.

The 1958 Convention of the High Seas in Geneva addressed radioactive waste:

ARTICLE 25

Every State shall take measures to prevent pollution of the seas from the dumping of radioactive waste, taking into account any standards and regulations which may be formulated by the competent international organizations.

All States shall cooperate with the competent international organizations in taking measures for the prevention of pollution of the seas or air space above, resulting from any activities with radioactive materials or other harmful agents.[87]

The U.S. Navy needed to find this torpedo and find it quick. The Geneva Convention authorized the hot pursuit of foreign ships in the territorial waters of another. The team needed to get in and get out as fast as possible without being detected.

The EOD team met with the captain of the ship and discussed the details of the mission. Once an EOD team puts their feet on deck, they are the most important men aboard.

The safety of the entire crew is in their hands. The men returned to the small craft boat.

Turner gave the order for Kelly and Byrd to execute search plan one alpha. The two divers hit the water. Byrd armed with the render safe device and Kelly, the sonar locator. The depth of the torpedo was unknown. After swimming for 20 minutes, the sonar locator found the torpedo. Byrd examined the torpedo, counting the number of blades and feeling for the exploder. Once it was verified as a torpedo, Byrd motioned for Kelly to return to the surface. The render safe procedure is a one-man job. This eliminates the possibility of losing multiple lives. Byrd attached the render safe device and broke the explosive train. A flotation bladder then was attached to the torpedo.

Once initiated, the bladder filled up and floated the torpedo to the surface, similar to a hot air balloon. The team executed the search, render safe, and recovery process to perfection. A 99 percent correctly executed procedure would not be good enough. The torpedo would have exploded.

Once the mission was complete, Byrd searched out the young men aboard the ship. He answered the majority of their questions and encouraged them to continue to pursue their dreams. He let them know that all things were possible if they were willing to work at it. A successful career in the Navy was obtainable for each and every one of them.

Byrd checked to see what time it was. It was 11:00 p.m. Central Standard Time. Weez and the children were sleeping.

Rear Admiral Bassinger from Commander Minecraft Pacific Fleet generated a Letter of Commendation to be included in Turner's, Kelly's, and Byrd's service records. Letters of Commendation and Appreciation were few and far between for Negroes. Byrd did not take the success of his career for granted. He thanked God for what He was doing in his life. Byrd recalled, where God guides, He provides.

REQUALIFICATIONS

December 22 finally had come, and Byrd was officially on leave. As he drove home, he could envision himself in his favorite chair reading the newspaper and awaiting the patter of his children's feet as they ran to give their daddy a hug. It was the start of two weeks of leave and Sherman was determined to enjoy every minute of it. Weez had a "honey-do" list waiting for him at the apartment, but they both agreed that he would take the first three days of leave to unwind and do absolutely nothing.

Sherman had learned from past vacations that it takes one or two days just to shake off the automatic motions of going to work each day. Besides, Saturday was his son's birthday, and he was looking forward to a time of celebration. Sherman Jr. would be turning nine years old. Recently, his son had started to complain about being the only man in the house. Sherman laughed out loud, "a ha, ha, ha." Every time he left the house, he would tell Sherman Jr., to be on his best behavior and look out for his mom and the girls while he was gone. There were quite a few girls, five to be exact. It was difficult to put into words the way Sherman felt about his daughters. It was much easier to describe the consequences one would suffer if they harmed them in any way. Every time he returned from a six-month cruise, he would bring home the biggest doll babies he could find. The tradition caused him to be the center of many jokes aboard the ship. His shipmates called him Santa Claus, and a few other things that he did not care to repeat. He would endure just about anything to be rewarded with the smiles he received from the girls. Some of the crew would ask him why he had so many children, and he would promptly respond, "I am trying to raise my own fleet!" while flashing a big, wide smile. So much about his family made him smile.

The last seven years of Sherman's life had been filled with many sobering thoughts and serious situations. Being a Navy diver was a relentless cycle of crisis situations. Lost bombs, downed planes, and ships in distress all were part of his job assignments. He often rotated between serving as a boatswain's mate, deep-sea diver, SCUBA diver, EOD, special weapons disposal, or any combination of the above.

Sherman had to stay abreast of all of the latest techniques and gadgets. Most of his free time was spent with his head buried deep in books studying. The diver career field was a heavy sea-duty occupation. He would be at sea two to three times longer than other sailors. Diver rotation was six years of sea duty, three years of shore duty. Sherman served 12 years of sea duty before he got his first shore-duty assignment. The constant requalification every six months kept the divers abreast of all of the new techniques other countries were using to disguise bombs. Some bombs were disguised as children's toys, a doll baby, or tanker truck. He was disarming bombs in his sleep. Two weeks of vacation would do him some good.

On January 6, 1962, Sherman reported back to NAVSCOLEOD at U.S. Naval Propellant Plant, Indian Head, Maryland. In five days he would be starting a six-week refresher course of instruction. Good news was floating around the school. Admiral Arleigh A. Burke, the chief of Naval Operations, authorized the formation of two unconventional warfare teams that had the capability to attack from the sea, air, or land. This small unit of 20 to 25 officers and 75 enlisted men were called SEALs, an acronym for sea, air, and land. SEAL Team ONE, assigned to the Pacific coast, and SEAL team TWO, the Atlantic coast, were formally established. The bulk of the 75 enlisted men came from the U.S. Navy UDT. Byrd had trained alongside some of them at Underwater Swimmers School down in Key West, Florida. The U.S. Navy EOD and SEALs are both combat swimmers.

On February 23, Sherman requalified as an EOD technician. The Navy made the switch from calling them EOD divers to EOD technicians because of the in-depth technical expertise required to disable bombs. Sherman progressed right from NAVSCOLEOD to the Nuclear Weapons Disposal School. The course encompassed chemical, biological, and nuclear warfare. On March 23, 1962, he successfully completed the course requalifying as a nuclear weapons disposal technician.

CHAPTER THIRTEEN

THE CUBAN MISSILE CRISIS

Byrd's three years of shore duty expired in April 1962, and he was ordered to report to *USS Wrangell* for duty as an EOD diver. *Wrangell* was serving outside of the continental United States. Byrd's current commitment to the U.S. Navy was about to expire in September. He and Weez had a lengthy discussion about whether or not he should reenlist. Their eldest child Sherlyn was 11 years old. Sherman had reservations about reenlisting with the children about to enter into their teenage years. If he reenlisted for six more years, he would have four teenagers in the house by the time it expired. This was a red flag in his mind, but on the other hand, he could retire at the end of his reenlistment commitment. Finally, after much conversation and prayer, they decided that he would reenlist.

In September 1962, with the recommendation of the boatswain's mate chief, the commanding officer of the *Wrangell* deemed Byrd worthy of reenlistment.

Byrd and Weez celebrated his reenlistment by purchasing a house at 1505 Cavalier Boulevard, Portsmouth, Virginia. Most days around 3:00 p.m., this was where he headed. his home, refuge, and castle. The single-family, red-brick, ranch-style home had three bedrooms, one bathroom, a living room, kitchen, dining room, and garage. He enjoyed lifting up the door of the garage and sitting in a lounge-type lawn chair as he watched the passing cars. They decided to purchase a home because it was becoming increasingly hard to find a landlord who would rent to a couple with six children.

Although he and Weez raised them to be respectful and well behaved, most landlords thought it was a front for the few minutes that the children were in their presence. Byrd took two weeks of leave from October 9 to October 23 to help Weez get things settled inside of the house. The twins had just celebrated their fifth birthday, and Weez baked them a cake as part of the celebration.

Sherman was grateful that Machinist Mate Chief Leonard King, a colored man who recently retired from the Navy, refused to rent them one side of a duplex he owned. He told Sherman that his income and credit qualified him to purchase a home. Sherman and Weez had just discussed buying a home during one of their late-night snacks at the kitchen table. They made plans to purchase within a year. Sometimes God answers a prayer while it is yet just a passing thought. Sherman was skilled at watching and praying for opportunity. The words of his English teacher at Stone Street High School were embedded deep down in his soul. Years of taking advantage of opportunities as they came had never dulled the praise he rendered to God for each and every one of them. Sherman remembered that opportunity is the appointed time of an event, pre- planned by Almighty God. It requires an act of faith. When the window opens, jump through it! Cavalier Manor was a recently built Negro neighborhood composed of brick residential homes in Portsmouth, Virginia. Chief King lived in the neighborhood and arranged for them to meet the realtor who sold him the house. Weez asked about the school zone. The neighborhood was zoned to attend one of the best colored schools in the city, Cavalier Manor Elementary. Weez was instantly sold. Race relations had improved a lot since Sherman joined the Navy, but white people still did not want Negroes living in the same neighborhood as they did. They wanted Negro men, in particular, to be as far away from their wives and daughters as possible.

There was something different about being a chief. The adage, once a chief, always a chief, was true. At work or home, chiefs felt a responsibility to mentor and teach younger enlisted sailors.

While enjoying time off, Sherman and Weez had the opportunity to invite the neighbors over for dinner. Joe and Marion Whitaker had five children who ranged in age right along with their own six children, 4 through 13 years old. The children walked to school together in the morning and played together in the evening. Marion and Weez hit it off well right from the start. They were both homemakers. Joe was a merchant seaman, and he and Sherman would sit and talk for hours. Well, Joe would talk for hours; Sherman did more listening than talking. Weez occasionally would hear Sherman say, "Is that right?" in that familiar calm tone of his. Sherman rarely talked about what he did in the Navy.

Weez's dining room table had six chairs, so she and Marion fed the kids first, the youngest to the oldest. When they had been children, things were just the opposite. The parents ate first, the children last. Most parents worked so hard in the field; the wives had to make sure they got enough nourishment to endure the rigors of the next day.

Weez and Marion fixed two rounds of dinner plates for their 11 children, six in the first round and five in the second. The children quickly ate the food so they could go back outside to play.

Just as the men were making their way to the dining room table, Sherman excused himself and headed toward the hallway as if he were going to the bathroom. As he passed by, he gave her an old familiar glance that she had come to love and hate at the same time. That little black gadget he carried around had alerted him to check in with his chain of command. Something important, something urgent was about to go down. She never knew how it worked. Did it ring, did it vibrate, or did it heat up? A call for him was a call for her. Years of experience trained her to execute a routine. She mustered up a smile and engaged Marion and Joe in conversation. Weez thought about how she would explain to the kids that daddy had to go away for a few days as she passed around the fried chicken, collard greens, and macaroni and cheese. They were supposed to be going on a family outing to the beach in the morning.

Sherman promptly reported to work; the Wrangell EOD team assembled in the briefing room. It was October 21, 1962. Six days earlier, a U.S. U-2 spy plane spotted a Soviet SS-4 medium-range ballistic missile being assembled for installation. Multiple sites were discovered. The pilot took pictures of the missile sites, and on October 16, the photos reached the hands of the president of the United States. An executive committee was formed to decide a plan of action quickly. If assembled and launched, the missiles had the capability to reach as far west as California and cause unheard-of destruction. This situation could very well be the beginning of a nuclear war!

Attempts to verbally resolve the crisis between the United States and Russia were unsuccessful. President John F. Kennedy ordered a quarantine of the waterways to Cuba to keep Russian ships from delivering more missiles. It was specifically labeled quarantine rather than naval blockade. Naval blockades were considered acts of war, and the President still hoped to avoid the use of nuclear weapons by either side.

USS Independence (CVA 62) the fourth ship in the Forrestal class of aircraft carriers was ordered to the region. Wrangell, an ammunition ship, also reported to the region for the loading of weapons onto vessels. Byrd was an expert in conventional, biological, chemical, and nuclear weapons disposal. Only the best EOD technicians were selected to train in nuclear weapons disposal. His experience as a boatswain's mate proved crucial in accomplishing the tasks needed on the ship in light of the crisis. He would be a part of a team that would oversee the transfer of nuclear weapons to the Independence. Time was of essence.

When Captain George Emerson Mason, the commanding officer of the Wrangell was ordered to deploy immediately in support of the quarantine of Cuban waterways, the ship departed Norfolk Naval Shipyard, Portsmouth, Virginia, with only half of the crew. The other half of the crew was on leave.[88] BM1 Byrd was one of those crewmembers on leave. He lived approximately 20 minutes away from the shipyard. Byrd kept a packed duffle bag ready at all times. As an EOD technician, he never knew when a situation would occur, and he would have to leave immediately. Such was the case on October 21, 1962. Byrd made it to the ship within an hour of being notified to return. Sherman and Weez never spent time on long goodbyes. They preferred it that way. She understood the part she played in support of the freedom of the country. She and Sherman were a team, and they complemented each other well. He would not have been able to focus as he needed to if he did not know that everything was going well at home. Weez kept the house in order, the kids fed and happy, and the bills paid. After all of that, she still had enough energy to be the friend and lover that he needed. Weez was a faithful partner, and she knew that he loved her very much. A kiss and a "see you later," and Byrd was gone.

Wrangell was ordered to the Caribbean. The ship armed and rearmed other vessels that participated in the naval quarantine, including Independence. A crisis was in the air.

The intensity of the situation was immense. Wrangell EOD team stood right in the thick of things, supporting operations around the clock. All the practice and intense physical training that Chief Harry Davis held them to on a daily basis were needed. Wrangell was battle ready.

The world's two superpowers, the United States and Russia, publicly made a deal to resolve the crisis. Russia agreed to remove all missiles from Cuba, and the United States vowed not to invade Cuba.[89] World War III was averted. Wrangell remained in the Caribbean for 35 days. The Cuban Missile Crisis had ended, but the nuclear arms race had just begun.

CHAPTER FOURTEEN

CHIEF IN HIS GRASP

President John F. Kennedy was determined to be prepared for the next possible confrontation. Whether it was Russia, China, Cuba, or some other country, the United States would be ready. First on the agenda was to win the nuclear arms race. The nation would build more weapons and train more people. The president would not rest until he was assured of the country's ability to defend itself. The president's mandate fueled the need for more people to serve the nation with skills such as those Byrd already had developed. The U.S. Armed Forces required more EOD technicians.

As Byrd examined his life, he could see the hand of God, crafting and weaving His will into being. Everything seemed clear to him now. He had taken advantage of most of the opportunities God presented through-out the years. Although he had missed some of them, he never missed God's purpose for his life. On May 16, 1963, Byrd advanced to Boatswain's Mate Chief. The anchor was now on his hat. Moreover, the anchor was in his heart.

Byrd remembered how he had watched the ships as they sailed up and down the Tallahatchie River. The different size anchors, in various stages of maintenance and decay, all had one thing in common. They had steadied the ship. They had fulfilled their God-given purpose. To Byrd, that was the most important aspect of life, fulfilling God's divine purpose.

Recalling how it was the anchor on the Navy recruiter's hat that had caught his attention on that September day at Stone Street High School, Byrd smiled. It had been the first time he had come in contact with a U.S. Navy chief. Byrd always would be indebted to the integrity displayed by Chief Johnson as he orchestrated the voluntary enlistment of a 17-year old apprentice. Ever since that day, Byrd felt as if he had been called to be a chief. Things had finally come full circle, and Byrd was right where God intended him to be.

The U.S. Navy's Bluejacket's Manual made it entirely clear that the rate of E-7 chief was attainable for each and every sailor who signed on the dotted line. Whether or not he advanced to that level was totally up to him. Byrd was glad that he was not stubborn. He always kept the advice of his brother Henry, front and center: "Find out what is required of you, and do it." After nearly 16 years of dedicated service, Byrd finally placed the cap with the anchor atop his head.

Sherman and Henry Byrd
Photo Courtesy of the Byrd Family

The chiefs who Byrd had encountered during his life set examples for him to follow. Chief Gray taught him about the pride of wearing a Navy uniform, showing him the correct posture and eye contact to be maintained while wearing it. Gray also laid out the road map for him to follow on his quest to become a chief. Calling things exactly the way he saw them, his assessment of Byrd's abilities significantly contributed to the U.S. Navy Diver programs.

Chief Stukes swiftly brought the wayward actions of his white petty officers and seaman back in line when they refused to train Byrd. He did not pretend that he did not see what was happening. The chief knew that festering blisters eventually pop. Stukes stripped them of their weekend liberty until all became compliant with the Navy's mandate for training junior sailors, Negro or white. Each sailor must be battle ready.

Chief Moore ensured that the officer over him knew the sacrifices and contributions his petty officers made toward the ship obtaining the coveted Battle E award for fulfilled mission goals, excellence in ship-handling, tactics, and weapon employment. Byrd received a Letter of Commendation and a Letter of Appreciation from his captain during his tour of duty on *Smalley*. Chief Moore had encouraged him to stick with his plan to become a Navy diver, and Byrd volunteered for Deep Sea Diver School.

Chief Walton exemplified integrity and professionalism. He did not allow the ill-willed traditions of the Navy, or his family, to skew his judgment of Byrd's character and ability to succeed as a deep sea diver. Pushing past his personal prejudices, Walton's focus remained on the mission.

Chief Calloway kept his eyes wide open and his ears to the ground to ensure that his sailors fared well at work and home. They were family, and he made sure the sailors knew he cared not only about them but also about their wives and children.

Chief Kelly was the epitome of a subject matter expert. Byrd learned so much about EOD under his leadership. Kelly was Byrd's sea daddy. The real meaning of "ask the chief" came alive in his presence. Byrd put in motion the things required of a chief under Kelly's watchful eye of instruction.

Chief King proved the adage that states "once a chief, always a chief" holds true even after retirement. If a chief can save a sailor some time, money, hard labor, or heartache, he will not hesitate to impart his wisdom and knowledge. Buying the house allowed Sherman and Weez to provide a stable home for their children. No matter where Byrd relocated, Weez and the children did not have to travel anymore. They could stay at home.

Chief Davis ensured that the Wrangell EOD team stayed battle ready. Under his leadership, the team practiced executing different procedures every day. Physical training was hellacious, but the team remained focused. Thanks to Davis, they were prepared to accomplish the mission in the time of war.

Now, it was Byrd's turn to execute the duties and responsibilities of a chief. As a first class petty officer, Byrd received plenty of practice. He knew this was the beginning of a higher level of commitment to the officers and sailors he would serve. Byrd was determined to uphold the honor, morality, and virtue embedded in a chief.

Boatswain's Mate Chief Sherman Byrd
Photo Courtesy of the Byrd Family

BIBLIOGRAPHY

1   Pilgram, Dr. David, Professor of Sociology. "What was Jim Crow." Jim Crow Museum: Origins of Jim Crow. September 2000. Accessed July 13, 2017. http://www.ferris.edu/jimcrow/what.htm.

2   Directorate, Navy Production. "All Hands Magazine Archive." All Hands 1947. 2017. Accessed July 13, 2017. http://www.navy.mil/ah_online/department_arch1947.html.

3   History.com Staff. "Truman signs the National Security Act." History.com. 2009. Accessed July 13, 2017. http://www.history.com/this-day-in-history/truman-signs-the-national-security-act.

4   "Navy Recruitment Poster Pay $75 a Month? -." Etsy. Accessed July 13, 2017. https://images.search.yahoo.com/yhs/search;_ylt=A0LEVigchjdZp9sAgf8PxQt.?p=navy%2Brecruitment%2Bposter%2Bpay%2B%2475%2Ba%2Bmnth%3F&fr=yhs-blp-default&fr2=piv-web&hspart=blp&hsimp=yhs-default&type=hmp_991_692_0#id=0&iurl=https%3A%2F%2Fimg0.etsystatic.com%2F000%2F0%2F6556552%2Fil_fullxfull.293281718.jpg&action=click.

5   Pilgram, Dr. David, Professor of Sociology. " What was Jim Crow." Jim Crow Museum: Origins of Jim Crow. September 2000. Accessed July 13, 2017. http://www.ferris.edu/jimcrow/what.htm.

6   Grimalkin, RN. "The History of Breastfeeding Among Black Women – What White Nurses Need to Know." Ofcourseitsaboutyou. March 10, 2014. Accessed July 13, 2017. https://ofcourseitsaboutyou.com/2014/03/10/the-history-of-breastfeeding-among-black-women-what-white-nurses-need-to-know/.

7   "Opportunity." Merriam-Webster.com. Merriam-Webster, n.d. Web. 13 July 2017. https://www.merriam-webster.com/dictionary/opportunity.

8   "The Chief's Fouled Anchor." Welcome to the Goatlocker. Accessed July 13, 2017. http://www.goatlocker.org/cpo.html.

9   Ibid

10 "Lynching Statistics." Lynching Statistics for 1882-1968. Accessed July 13, 2017. http://www.chesnuttarchive.org/classroom/lynchingstat.html.

11 "Disasters." NYCdata: The Blizzard of 1947. Accessed July 13, 2017. http://www.baruch.cuny.edu/nycdata/disasters/blizzards-1947.html.

12 "Weather Almanac for KGWO - December, 1947." Weather Underground (10.226.234.236). Accessed July 13, 2017. https://www.wunderground.com/history/airport/KGWO/1947/12/26/DailyHistory.html?req_city=&req_state=&req_stat-

ename=&reqdb.zip=&reqdb.magic=&reqdb.wmo=.

13   "Slave Life on a Cotton Plantation, 1845." Slave Life on a Cotton Plantation, 1845. Accessed July 13, 2017. http://college.cengage.com/history/ayers_primary_sources/slave_life_cotton_plantation.htm.

14   Byrd, Ned. (Brother of Sherman Byrd), in discussion with author. September 2009

15   "Resistance." National Great Blacks In Wax Museum. May 16, 2005. Accessed July 13, 2017. http://www.greatblacksinwax.org/Exhibits/lynching.htm.

16   Pilgram, Dr. David, Professor of Sociology. " What was Jim Crow." Jim Crow Museum: Origins of Jim Crow. September 2000. Accessed July 13, 2017. http://www.ferris.edu/jimcrow/what.htm.

17   "Resistance." National Great Blacks In Wax Museum. May 16, 2005. Accessed July 13, 2017. http://www.greatblacksinwax.org/Exhibits/lynching.htm.

18   Directorate, Navy Production. "All Hands Magazine Archive." All Hands 1947. 2017. Accessed July 13, 2017. http://www.navy.mil/ah_online/department_arch1947.html.

19   San Diego Naval Historical Association. "Navy Training Center." Naval Training Center, San Diego. Accessed July 13, 2017. http://www.militarymuseum.org/NTCSanDiego.html.

20   Google Search. Accessed July 13, 2017. https://www.google.com/search?q=sign%2Breads%2Byou%2Bare%2Bnow%2Bmen%2Bof%2Bthe%-2BUnited%2BStates%2BNavy%2Bsan%2Bdiego%2Bcalifornia%2Bnavy%2B-training%2Bcenter%3F&source=lnms&tbm=isch&sa=X&ved=0ahUKEwjwhtv-pZDU-AhVmwYMKHfbOAfQQ_AUICigB&biw=1600&bih=794#imgrc=1hKilyCQVzYCIM:.

21   Pilgram, Dr. David, Professor of Sociology. " What was Jim Crow." Jim Crow Museum: Origins of Jim Crow. September 2000. Accessed July 13, 2017. http://www.ferris.edu/jimcrow/what.htm

22   Byrd, Ned. (Brother of Sherman Byrd), in discussion with author. September 2009

23   "A. Philip Randolph." Encyclopædia Britannica. Accessed July 13, 2017. https://www.britannica.com/biography/A-Philip-Randolph.

24   Cutler, Thomas J. "The Bluejackets' manual : Cutler, Thomas J., 1947- : Free Download & Streaming." Internet Archive. 1998. Accessed July 13, 2017. https://archive.org/details/bluejacketsmanu00navygoog.

25   Ibid

26   Byrd, Ned. (Brother of Sherman Byrd), in discussion with author. September 2009

27   Cutler, Thomas J. "The Bluejackets' manual : Cutler, Thomas J., 1947- : Free Download & Streaming." Internet Archive. 1998. Accessed July 13, 2017. https://archive.org/details/bluejacketsmanu00navygoog.

28   Ibid

29   "Harry S. Truman Library & Museum." Truman Library - Executive Order 9981. 2017. Accessed July 13, 2017. https://www.trumanlibrary.org/9981.htm.

30 "Navy CyberSpace." Rating. December 21, 2016. Accessed July 13, 2017. https://www.navycs.com/navy-jobs/personnel-specialist.html.

31 USS Tarawa (CV 40) history. 2010. Accessed July 13, 2017. http://www.uscarriers.net/cv40history.htm.

32 Cutler, Thomas J. "The Bluejackets' manual : Cutler, Thomas J., 1947- : Free Download & Streaming." Internet Archive. 1998. Accessed July 13, 2017. https://archive.org/details/bluejacketsmanu00navygoog.

33 "USNI Logo." The Role of the Chief Petty Officer in the Modern Navy | U.S. Naval Institute. Accessed July 13, 2017. https://www.usni.org/magazines/proceedings/1957-04/role-chief-petty-officer-modern-navy.

34 Ibid

35 "Naval Base History." Naval Base History - North Charleston. Accessed July 13, 2017. http://www.northcharleston.org/Visitors/Attractions/Greater-Charleston-Naval-Base-Memorial/Naval-Base-History.aspx.

36 Williams, Paul "Hucklebuck" (1915–2002) | The Black Past: Remembered and Reclaimed. Accessed July 13, 2017. http://www.blackpast.org/aah/williams-paul-hucklebuck-1915-2002.

37 "History of the Cha Cha Dance." Dance America, Inc. Accessed July 13, 2017. http://www.dance-america.com/history-of-the-cha-cha-dance-81.html.

38 "Korean War." Encyclopædia Britannica. Accessed July 13, 2017. https://www.britannica.com/event/Korean-War.

39 "US Navy Traditions, Customs, & Core Values." US Navy Traditions, Customs, & Core Values : Navy.com. Accessed July 13, 2017. https://www.navy.com/about/tradition.

40 "President Truman receives NSC-68." History.com. Accessed July 13, 2017. http://www.history.com/this-day-in-history/president-truman-receives-nsc-68.

41 Lab, Digital Scholarship. "The History Engine." History Engine: Tools for Collaborative Education and Research | Episodes. Accessed July 13, 2017. https://historyengine.richmond.edu/episodes/view/4682.

42 "USNI Logo." The Role of the Chief Petty Officer in the Modern Navy | U.S. Naval Institute. Accessed July 13, 2017. https://www.usni.org/magazines/proceedings/1957-04/role-chief-petty-officer-modern-navy.

43 "Harry S. Truman Library & Museum." Truman Library - Records of the President's Committee on Equality of Treatment and Opportunity in the Armed Services. Accessed July 13, 2017. https://www.trumanlibrary.org/hstpaper/fahy.htm.

44 "Truman relieves MacArthur of duties in Korea." History.com. Accessed July 13, 2017. http://www.history.com/this-day-in-history/truman-relieves-macarthur-of-duties-in-korea.

45 "Biography, Matthew B. Ridgway." Matthew B Ridgway. Accessed July 13, 2017. http://www.nj.gov/military/korea/biographies/ridgway.html.

46 Byrd, Ned. (Brother of Sherman Byrd), in discussion with author. September 2009.

47   "Rate Insignia of Navy Enlisted Personnel." U.S. Navy Ranks - Enlisted. 2009. Accessed July 13, 2017. http://www.navy.mil/navydata/ranks/rates/rates.html.

48   Cutler, Thomas J. "The Bluejackets' manual : Cutler, Thomas J., 1947- : Free Download & Streaming." Internet Archive. 1998. Accessed July 13, 2017. https://archive.org/details/bluejacketsmanu00navygoog

49   Sierra, Jerry A. "Notes on Guantánamo Bay." Historical Look at Guantanamo. Accessed July 13, 2017. http://www.historyofcuba.com/history/funfacts/guantan.htm.

50   Scott D. Fell, DO, FAAEM. "The Bends: Decompression Sickness from Scuba Diving." EMedicineHealth. Accessed July 14, 2017. http://www.emedicinehealth.com/decompression_syndromes_the_bends/article_em.htm.

51   Alex McBride. "Brown vs Board of Education." PBS. December 2006. Accessed July 14, 2017. http://www.pbs.org/wnet/supremecourt/rights/landmark_brown.html.

52   1st Class Daniel Garas. "Silent Professionals: History of the Rank of Chief Petty Officer." Navy Live. March 31, 2015. Accessed July 14, 2017. http://navylive.dodlive.mil/2015/03/31/happy-122nd-birthday-chief-petty-officers/.

53   "BibleGateway." Isaiah 26:3 KJV - - Bible Gateway. Accessed July 14, 2017. https://www.biblegateway.com/passage/?search=I saiah% 2B26%3A3&version=KJV.

54   "10 U.S. Code § 815 - Art. 15. Commanding officer's non-judicial punishment." LII / Legal Information Institute. Accessed July 14, 2017. https://www.law.cornell.edu/uscode/text/10/815.

55   Chief Personnelman Don A, Kelso, U. S. Navy. "The Role of the Chief Petty Officer in the Modern Navy | U.S. Naval Institute." The Role of the Chief Petty Officer in the Modern Navy | U.S. Naval Institute. Accessed July 14, 2017. https://www.usni.org/magazines/proceedings/1957-04/role-chief-petty-officer-modern-navy.

56   "10 U.S. Code § 815 - Art. 15. Commanding officer's non-judicial punishment." LII / Legal Information Institute. Accessed July 14, 2017. https://www.law.cornell.edu/uscode/text/10/815.

57   Chief Personnelman Don A, Kelso, U. S. Navy. "The Role of the Chief Petty Officer in the Modern Navy | U.S. Naval Institute." The Role of the Chief Petty Officer in the Modern Navy | U.S. Naval Institute. Accessed July 14, 2017. https://www.usni.org/magazines/proceedings/1957-04/role-chief-petty-officer-modern-navy.

58   Byrd, Ned. (Brother of Sherman Byrd), in discussion with author. September 2009

59   Adcristal. "U.S. Navy Mark V Deep Diving Suit at the U.S. Navy Museum." Flickr. June 21, 2009. Accessed July 14, 2017. https://www.flickr.com/photos/adcristal/3645045985.

60   Smith, Stew. "Where Did the Term 'Hooah' Come From?" The Balance. Accessed July 14, 2017. https://www.thebalance.com/origins-of-hoo.

61   History.com Staff. "The death of Emmett Till." History.com. 2010. Accessed July 14, 2017. http://www.history.com/this-day-in-history/the-death-of-emmett-till.

62   History.com Staff. "Rosa Parks." History.com. 2009. Accessed July 14, 2017. http://www.history.com/topics/black-history/rosa-parks.

63 Christensen, Stephanie. "The Great Migration (1915-1960)." The Great Migration (1915-1960) | The Black Past: Remembered and Reclaimed. Accessed July 14, 2017. http://www.blackpast.org/aah/great-migration-1915-1960.

64 "USS Nantahala." USS Nantahala. Accessed July 14, 2017. http://www.nantahalanc. com/untitled2.html.

65 "Fraternal Order of Underwater Swimmers School." U.S. Navy Underwater Swimmers School. Accessed July 14, 2017. http://www.uwss.org/SchoolHistory1970.html.

66 Directorate, Navy Production. "All Hands Magazine Archive." All Hands 1947. 2017. Accessed July 13, 2017. http://www.navy.mil/ah_online/department_arch1947.html.

67 Ibid

68 Ibid

69 "USNI Logo." The Role of the Chief Petty Officer in the Modern Navy | U.S. Naval Institute. Accessed July 14, 2017. https://www.usni.org/magazines/proceedings/1957-04/ role-chief-petty-officer-modern-navy.

70 Chief Personnelman Don A, Kelso, U. S. Navy. "The Role of the Chief Petty Officer in the Modern Navy | U.S. Naval Institute." The Role of the Chief Petty Officer in the Modern Navy | U.S. Naval Institute. Accessed July 14, 2017. https://www.usni.org/ magazines/proceedings/1957-04/role-chief-petty-officer-modern-navy.

71 "Motto of the Ordnance EOD unit: - Page 2." Motto of the Ordnance EOD unit: - Forum Page 2. Accessed July 14, 2017. https://www.military-quotes.com/forum/motto-ordnance-eod-unit-page2-t462.html.

72 Ibid

73 "Old School EOD Movie." Old School EOD Movie - SOCNET: The Special Operations Community Network. Accessed July 14, 2017. http://www.socnet.com/show-thread.php?t=105239.

74 "Motto of the Ordnance EOD unit: - Page 2." Motto of the Ordnance EOD unit: - Forum Page 2. Accessed July 14, 2017. http://www.military-quotes.com/forum/motto-ordnance-eod-unit-page2-t462.html.

75 SGM Mike R.Vining, USA (Retired). "PVT Michael Costagliola." EOD Warrior Foundation. Accessed July 14, 2017. http://www.eodwarriorfoundation.org/memorial/warrior/michael-costagliola.

76 "NavSource Online: Aircraft Carrier Photo Archive." Aircraft Carrier Photo Index: USS RANDOLPH (CV-15). Accessed July 14, 2017. http://www.navsource.org/archives/02/15.htm.

77 "Fulgencio Batista." Encyclopædia Britannica. Accessed July 14, 2017. https://www. britannica.com/biography/Fulgencio-Batista.

78 Sierra, Jerry A. "Batista." Fulgencio Batista, from army sergeant to dictator. Accessed July 14, 2017. http://www.historyofcuba.com/history/batista.htm.

79 McKelvey, Charles. "Fidel: History Will Absolve Me." Global Learning. August 16, 2014. Accessed July 14, 2017. http://www.globallearning-cuba.com/blog-umlthe-view-

from-the-southuml/fidel-history-will-absolve-me.

80 Mc Kelvey, Charles. "Fidel Castro born." History.com. Accessed July 14, 2017. http://www.history.com/this-day-in-history/fidel-castro-born.

81 "Fidel Castro." Biography.com. April 28, 2017. Accessed July 14, 2017. https://www.biography.com/people/fidel-castro-9241487.

82 Andrews, Evan. "Fidel Castro's Wild New York Visit." History.com. September 18, 2015. Accessed July 14, 2017. http://www.history.com/news/fidel-castros-wild-new-york-visit-55-years-ago.

83 "The Bay of Pigs Invasion." Central Intelligence Agency. April 18, 2016. Accessed July 14, 2017. https://www.cia.gov/news-information/featured-story-archive/2016-featured-story-archive/the-bay-of-pigs-invasion.html.

84 Directorate, Navy Production. "History of the Chief Petty Officer Grade." All Hands Department : History and Heritage. Accessed July 14, 2017. http://www.navy.mil/ah_online/deptStory.asp?dep=8&id=73147.

85 Johnson, T. "Naval History: Honoring John Henry ("Dick") Turpin, Chief Gunner's Mate, USN. (1876-1962)." Navy Live. February 23, 2011. Accessed July 14, 2017. http://navylive.dodlive.mil/2011/02/23/naval-historyhonoring-john-henry-dick-turpin-chief-gunners-mate-usn-1876-1962/.

86 "History of the CPO Charge Book." History of the CPO Charge Book. Accessed July 14, 2017. http://www.goatlocker.org/resources/cpo/history/charge.htm.

87 "Convention On the High Seas." Index of /documents. Accessed July 14, 2017. http://www.gc.noaa.gov/documents.

88 "Genesis of the U.S. Navy's Sea, Air, Land (SEAL) Teams | National Navy UDT-SEAL Museum." National Navy SEAL Museum. Accessed July 14, 2017. https://www.navy-sealmuseum.org/about-navy-seals/genesis-u-s-navys-sea-air-land-seal-teams.

89 "The World On the Brink." Cuban Missile Crisis - John F. Kennedy Presidential Library & Museum. Accessed July 14, 2017. http://microsites.jfklibrary.org/cmc/oct20/.

90 Ibid

AUTHOR AFFILIATIONS

Cynthia Byrd Conner is the daughter of Sherman and Louise Byrd. Recently retired, she was employed by the Department of the Navy, Naval Sea Systems Command, Southeast Regional Maintenance Center as a Management and Program Analyst in the Engineering Department. She has over 25 years of experience in ship maintenance and repair. A graduate of Florida State College at Jacksonville (FSCJ), Cindy completed the Bachelor of Applied Science degree in Supervision and Management. FSCJ has a rich history of supporting our military community. The Military and Veteran's Service Center provides assistance and referral services to active military, veterans, and their family members, ensuring academic success.

Cindy is a member of the Organization of Black Maritime Graduates, a 501(c)(3) organization that educates, mentors, and provides scholarships for minorities from all over the world to attend the State University of New York Maritime College.

She is also a member of the Florida Writers Association and the Military Writers Society of America.

Married to Alton M. Conner Sr. for over thirty years, they continue to joyfully strive to fulfill God's will for their lives. God has blessed them with a daughter, son, son-in-law, and granddaughter. They all reside in the beautiful city of Jacksonville, Florida.

You may contact Cindy at Cynthia Byrd Conner, 731 Duval Station Road, Suite 107-155, Jacksonville, FL 32218. cynthiaconner1957@gmail.com. 904-704-4727.

For more information about Cynthia Byrd Conner or Quiet Strong, please visit www.quietstrong.com